INTERNATIONAL DEVELOPMENT IN FOCUS

Ideas for Action 2019

Financing and Implementing Sustainable Development

Mahmoud Mohieldin and Djordjija Petkoski, Editors

Contents

CHAPTER 7   **Fresh Water and Ice Solution for Fishing Communities on Remote Islands of Indonesia   81**
Shana Fatina, Atiek Puspa Fadhilah, and Fakhri Guniar

Figures

Tables

Preface

We are pleased to present the winners of the 2019 Ideas for Action (I4A) competition, an initiative in which young people submit their proposals for implementing the Sustainable Development Goals (SDGs). I4A was launched in November 2014 by the World Bank Group and the Zicklin Center for Business Ethics Research at the Wharton School of the University of Pennsylvania. This year's winners were selected from more than 3,000 proposals, which included over 21,000 participants from 142 countries—a 50 percent increase in proposals over 2018.

The SDGs are a holistic and urgent call for global action and partnerships that address a wide range of interconnected issues. The 17 goals of the 2030 Agenda for Sustainable Development include ending poverty, improving health and education, reducing inequality, confronting climate change, and many others. Adopted by the United Nations General Assembly in September 2015, the SDGs present a more ambitious agenda than the Millennium Development Goals, which expired in 2015. Since nearly half of the world's population is under 25 years old, it is today's youth who will be tasked with realizing this grand vision.

Empowering young people to take action is fundamental to achieving the SDGs—and the I4A competition does exactly that. It engages and inspires young people from around the world to develop and share their ideas for implementing the 2030 Agenda by envisioning and designing solutions that can help reach the SDGs. Though it does not offer financial prizes, the competition gives winners an opportunity to meet and discuss their work with leading professionals in the global development industry and the private sector.

This year's competition received a record number of participants, with the highest number of participants coming from Brazil, Colombia, the Arab Republic of Egypt, India, Indonesia, Mozambique, Nigeria, Tanzania, and Uganda.

The winning proposals went through a rigorous selection process based on the criteria of depth and clarity, significance of impact, originality and creativity, and feasibility. The teams had to showcase a strong and clear proposal that demonstrates potential for benefiting a large number of people while presenting a practical roadmap for implementation. Reviewers included young staff members as well as executives from Firmenich, Flour Mills of Nigeria, the German–Brazilian Chamber of Commerce and Industry, PepsiCo, the Wharton School, and the World Bank Group. Other competition partners included the International Labour Organization,

Hemofarm, the World Bank Group's Youth to Youth (Y2Y) Community and Youth Summit, Knowledge@Wharton, and the United Nations Youth Assembly.

The 2019 winners will present their proposals at the World Bank Group and International Monetary Fund Annual Meetings in October 2019 in Washington, DC and at other high-level international events. The Wharton School will also offer the winners opportunities for training and knowledge exchange.

WINNING PROPOSALS

The 2019 winning proposal, by Team CareNX Innovations from India, addresses the problem of high neonatal morbidity and mortality in much of the country, to help achieve SDG 3 (ensure healthy lives and promote well-being for all at all ages). This team developed two interconnected, indigenous, and portable smartphone-enabled devices—Fetosense and U-Act—to monitor uterine contractions for early identification of and intervention with preterm labor in parts of the world that have few doctors and no equipment. The devices can share results remotely with the patient's gynecologist. This proposal could be used in conjunction with an existing CareNX program, called CareMother, in which local health workers use a portable diagnostic kit for antenatal tests to upload results to the cloud. Judges felt this proposal presented a strong case for the program's potential scalability to achieve the goal of improving health in underserved areas.

The second-place proposal, by Gather from the United Kingdom, addresses outbreaks of enteric and diarrheal disease by using geospatial data analysis to direct investments in sanitation to high-risk areas. This team produces geospatial sanitation flow diagrams. It has launched its services in Madagascar, the country rated fourth worst in the world for sanitation provision. This proposal addresses SDG 6 (clean water and sanitation) and suggests establishing sanitation data hubs and a global Sanitation Data Commission to complement and bolster its work. It also proposes partnerships with local governments and other organizations. Judges said this proposal showcased the power of technology and data to improve sanitation.

The third-place team, WellPower from Kenya, proposes a tech-enabled, vertically integrated clean water provider and distribution network to address the issue of inadequate access to clean water, which affects at least 350 million people in Sub-Saharan Africa and 19 million people in Kenya, the target country. Addressing SDG 6, it proposes installing and operating a solar-powered water filtration system in communities. The program uses a mobile app and SMS (texting) to match water customers with local delivery services that can provide clean water on demand. Judges felt this model enabled users to obtain clean water conveniently and affordably.

The Eco Panplas team from Brazil—one of the four runners-up in the competition—proposed a solution to the harmful effects of plastic packaging and the large amount of water needed to recycle plastic. This team has developed a decontamination and package-recycling technology that does not need water and creates no waste. The prototype has processed 8 million lubricating oil containers over the past two years, recovering and selling 400 tons of recycled plastic for new packaging and recovering 15,000 liters of oil for reuse. This technology addresses SDG 12 (responsible consumption and production patterns) through its innovative packaging solutions.

Ekomuro H$_2$0+ from Colombia, another runner-up, has produced a rainwater-harvesting technology made from reused polyethylene terephthalate (PET) bottles. PET is a raw material typically used to make plastic packaging materials for a wide range of consumer goods. PET bottles can be reused to create a vertical-type water tank that is compact and resistant to liquid pressures. The team aims to serve schools and homes by disseminating its idea to educational communities. It has already conducted outreach to 40 families in Comuna 4 and implemented the project in eight schools in Bogotá. This project aims to address SDG 6 (clean water and sanitation) by proposing a solution for urban communities to promote greater awareness of the advantages of rainwater collection.

DamoGO, another runner-up, from the Republic of Korea, tackles the problem of food waste through a mobile app that allows people to purchase and rescue good, unsold food before it is thrown away at the end of the day. The team partners with restaurants and food retailers so that users can search for and pick up discounted food—priced at least 50 percent below the original cost—by location or receive real-time notifications on the app. The DamoGO team has launched its platform in 15 stores in Seoul for beta testing and has reported profitable turnovers for each store. This innovative start-up profitably addresses SDG 2 (end hunger) and SDG 12 (sustainable consumption and production).

The fourth runner-up team, Komodo Water from Indonesia, introduces a solution for improving access to clean water and fresh fish supplies from the brackish water sources in the Paparang Islands and Komodo National Park in Indonesia. Through reverse osmosis and ice block machines, powered by solar energy, fishing communities are able to purify brackish water into drinking water and create ice to store their fish or use for other purposes. This project addresses SDG 6 (clean water and sanitation); SDG 7 (ensure access to affordable, reliable, sustainable, and modern energy); SDG 12 (sustainable consumption and production); SDG 14 (conserve and sustainably use the marine ecosystem); and SDG 8 (create opportunities for good and decent jobs and secure livelihoods).

Teams that won honorable mention are Community Health Leaders (Ukraine), E Vigilante (Bangladesh), Team Footmo (Uganda), Fresh Source (Egypt), Golden Banana Syrup (Indonesia), Good Waste (Jordan), Hilico (India), Irada (Egypt), Living Waters (India), Vinsighte (Nigeria), and WASE (Italy).

SUPPORTING THE FUTURE IMPLEMENTERS OF THE 2030 AGENDA FOR SUSTAINABLE DEVELOPMENT

The I4A competition is an innovative platform that allows young people to take ownership of the SDGs and gain access to key professionals in the global development industry and the private sector to help them launch their ideas for local and global impact. We hope this incubation process will enable these ideas to flourish and shape our shared future for the better, because youth participation is key to achieving the 2030 Agenda for Sustainable Development. The initiative also facilitates collaborative learning through a knowledge-sharing platform. By using new methods or technology to address SDG targets, young people can have a direct impact on their own communities and contribute to the global goals.

We have produced a series of engagement activities—including video-conferences, webcasts, blogs, and other shared resources—to engage the competition participants and others who are eager to take part in the global development conversation. The aim is to connect leading schools of finance and management, along with governments around the world, to build partnerships that shape ideas into effective implementation.

This book will allow the World Bank Group and other development partners to recognize the incredible talent and innovative spirit that these young people bring to the global development conversation—breaking away from existing development practice in pursuit of innovative and scalable approaches. We need their voices in the global development conversation, because only with their leadership and ideas can we create a brighter future for all.

Mahmoud Mohieldin
Senior Vice President for the 2030 Development Agenda,
UN Relations and Partnerships
World Bank Group

Djordjija Petkoski
Lecturer, Legal Studies and Business Ethics Department,
Wharton School, University of Pennsylvania

Acknowledgments

Ideas for Action (I4A) is a joint initiative of the World Bank Group (WBG) and the Zicklin Center for Business Ethics Research at the Wharton School of the University of Pennsylvania, in partnership with the WBG's Youth to Youth (Y2Y) Community and Youth Summit. Over the past five years, I4A has benefited from the commitment, support, and insightful feedback of the staff members of these organizations, as well as from the dedicated champions of the initiative.

At the WBG, this initiative was coordinated by Arunima Dhar, senior operations officer, Office of the Senior Vice President for the 2030 Development Agenda, United Nations Relations and Partnerships (SVPMM). The Wharton team was led by Dominic Johnson.

The I4A team members would especially like to acknowledge the World Bank Africa Region External Communications Team, led by Steven Shalita, for its outreach efforts in the region. We would like to thank the young professionals from these organizations as well as several other volunteers who took leadership roles in implementing the initiative.

The selection process comprised three phases. The following individuals conducted the first round of reviews, resulting in the selection of the first round of finalists: Farida Aboulmagd, Kehinde Ajuwon, Roman Alexander, Joanne Anand, Jaya Anderman, Mukose Andrew, Hillary Aristotle, Anita Avery, Chris Avery, Nicholas Bian, Bianca Cristina Butacu, Demet Cabbar, Lisa Castro, Estee Chen, Frances di Cristina, Monica Czucman, Devy Damayanti, Alima Diakite, Elke Esmeralda Dikoume, Anne Marie Gabrielle Dujour, Oana Frant, Marcellin Noudéhouénou Gandonou, Sander Glas, Sam Goidell, Julius Gwyer, Lobna Hadji, Angela Harding, Omar Ibn Abdillah, Koumba Ibouili, Michelle D Jaffee, Dominic Johnson, Elizabeth Johnson, Jim Johnson, Filip Jolevski, Léa Philippe Kagan, Sam Johninho Kalungi, Ning Li, Yani Li, Mariam Hoda El Maghrabi, Sarisha Maharaj, Melissa Marketos, Kevin Meehan, Jennifer Ann Melendez, Pallavi Menon, Saadique Merchant, Lais Miachon, Maha El Moaz, Djeanane Monfort, John K. Mulaa, Joel Kouadio Nda Ndri, Ferran Pérez, Alex Pio, Erick Rabemananoro, Sabhya Raju, Nora Ramadan, Sireesh Ramesh, Abirami Sadasivam, Joelle El Sawalhi, Nermeen Shahata, Rebecca Spriggs, Samuel Steven, Joud Tabaza, Aaditi Tamhankar, Nandjim Tchaalla, Yoelena Tkebuchava, David Tucker, Shivin Uppal, Ievgeniia Viatchaninova, Eman Wahby, and Agbannon Yves.

In the second round, which selected the 18 finalists, the submissions were reviewed by four expert groups chaired by Björn Gillsater, manager and special representative, SVPMM World Bank New York office; Djordjija Petkoski, lecturer and senior fellow, Wharton School; Marco Scuriatti, adviser, SVPMM, WBG; and Jaehyang So, senior adviser, SVPMM, WBG.

Group A was chaired by Marco Scuriatti and included Stathis Anagnostou, board adviser, Flour Mills of Nigeria; Filip Fidanoski, researcher, Luxembourg School of Finance and University of Luxembourg; Felipe Gonzalez, professor, Diego Portales University, Santiago, Chile; Daniel Lederman, lead economist, Middle East and North Africa, WBG; and Victor Gabriel de Oliveira Rodríguez, professor, University of São Paulo, Brazil.

Group B was chaired by Björn Gillsater and included Carolina Busco, professor, Diego Portales University, Santiago, Chile; Gustavo Diaz, professor, Diego Portales University, Santiago, Chile; Steven Dimitriyev lead specialist, Trade and Competitiveness Global Practice, WBG; Thomas Michael Kerr, manager, Global Engagement and Outreach, International Finance Corporation (IFC); and Maria Alejandra Gonzalez Perez, professor, Department of Organization and Management, EAFIT University, Medellín, Colombia.

Group C was chaired by Djordjija Petkoski and included Natalia Agapitova, senior economist, Trade and Competitiveness Global Practice, World Bank; Bryan Bloom, partner and CFO, ENODO; John Levy, director of impact, Franklin Templeton; Dragan Radic, head, Small and Medium Enterprises (SME) unit, International Labour Organization; Sanda Savic, director, Corporate Affairs and Communications Center; and Steven Shalita, manager, Office of the Chief Economist in the Africa Region, World Bank.

Group D was chaired by Jaehyang So, senior adviser, SVPMM, WBG, and included Jiten Agarwal, U.S. India Skills & Education Council, Cambridge Education Development, and Expedien, Inc.; Lisa A. Chase, communications strategist associated with HBS; Marko Jakovljevic, postdoctoral fellow, Stanford University; and Berangere Magarinos-Ruchat, vice president of sustainability at Firmenich.

The qualifying Spanish-language proposals were reviewed by Gabriela de la Garza, senior director for Latin America Beverages Corporate Affairs, Citizenship and Sustainability, PepsiCo Latin America; and Maria-Alejandra Gonzales-Perez, professor, Department of Organization and Management, EAFIT University. The qualifying French-language proposals were reviewed by Lwanzo Amani, Global CDL, and Berangere Magarinos-Ruchat, vice president of sustainability, Firmenich. The qualifying Arabic-language proposals were reviewed by M Saadique A Merchant, PricewaterhouseCoopers, Dubai, the United Arab Emirates; Maha el Moaz, team leader, GFA Consulting Group; and Nermeen Shehata, assistant professor of accounting, American University, Cairo. The qualifying Portuguese language proposals were reviewed by Eduardo Saad Diniz, professor, University of São Paulo; Bruno Vath Zarpellon, director, Department of Innovation and Technology, Chamber of Commerce and Industry, Brazil–Alemanha; and Rodolfo Walder Viana, head, BASF Foundation, Brazil.

The final round, which selected the winners, runners-up, and honorable mention awardees, was reviewed by Mahmoud Mohieldin, World Bank senior vice president for the 2030 Development Agenda, UN Relations and Partnerships, with Stathis Anagnostou, board adviser, Flour Mills of Nigeria; John Coumantaros, chairman, Flour Mills of Nigeria; Karin Finkelston, vice president, IFC Partnerships, Communications and Outreach; Hafez Ghanem, World

Bank vice president, Africa Region; Gilbert Ghostine, CEO, Firmenich; Tom Kerr, director, IFC; Luis Montoya, president, Latin America Beverages PepsiCo; Mukul Panday, editor-in-chief/executive director, Knowledge@Wharton; Djordjija Petkoski, lecturer and senior fellow, Wharton Business School; Nena Stoiljkovic, vice president, IFC; Thomas Timm, head, German Chamber of Commerce; and Marilou Uy, director, Intergovernmental Group of Twenty-Four on International Monetary Affairs and Development (G-24).

The book was edited by Marcy Gessel, Kathy Kelly, and Kay McCarthy of Publications Professionals LLC. The I4A team members would also like to thank Cindy Fisher and Janice Tuten for their excellent management of the publication process. A sincere thanks to Nidhi Rao, Tufts University, for her valuable help with the 2019 I4A initiative and the publication process.

Finally, a very special thanks to the over 21,000 young people who shared their innovative ideas in more than 3,000 proposals from 142 countries. Without their passion and energy, none of this would have been possible.

1 Fetosense and U-Act: Novel Solutions for Monitoring Fetal Heart Rate and Uterine Activity to Reduce Neonatal Morbidity and Mortality

SHANTANU PATHAK, *Chief executive officer*

ADITYA KULKARNI, *Chief technology officer*

AMEYA BONDRE, *Head, clinical research and development*

PRINCE NADAR, *Embedded hardware developer*

ROHIT SRIVASTAVA, *Head and professor, Department of Biosciences and Bioengineering, IIT-Bombay*

AVINASH JOSHI, *Software development lead*

ANJANA DONAKONDA, *Senior program manager*

ABSTRACT About 750,000 neonates die annually in India, and preterm birth contributes to 43 percent of neonatal deaths. Simple, accurate, and time- and cost-efficient labor-monitoring tools are scarce at the grassroots level, particularly for the estimated 150,000 subcenters manned by auxiliary nurse midwives. The current standard—cardiotocography—has poor accuracy and is bulky, difficult to use, expensive, sensitive to maternal obesity and movements, and not scalable.

CareNX Innovations has developed two interconnected, indigenous, and portable smartphone-enabled solutions: Fetosense, for fetal heart monitoring, and U-Act, for monitoring uterine contractions for early identification of and intervention for preterm labor. When used with our existing mobile maternal care program, CareMother—which involves doorstep antenatal tests conducted by frontline workers using a portable diagnostic kit, cloud-based data sharing, and a mobile application—both Fetosense and U-Act can provide an end-to-end solution for effective labor monitoring to reduce postnatal complications.

India reports 26 million viable pregnancies annually. Of those, 50–60 percent are estimated as high risk. They are served by an estimated 135,000 hospitals and

CareNX Innovations, India.

more than 300,000 clinics. As India has only 35,000 gynecologists, greater use of Fetosense and U-Act at these facilities would be beneficial. Results can be auto-interpreted using machine-learning algorithms, to correlate recurrent patterns in fetal heart rate and uterine activity with fetal cardiac function, metabolic acidosis, and neonatal outcomes. This will reduce the continuous dependence on the clinician and enable substantially greater use of remote monitoring by doctors.

PROBLEM AND CONTEXT

Monitoring labor is essential to track its progress, assess fetal heart rate, and measure uterine contractions to identify any excessive activity that may lead to adverse fetal outcomes (Ayres-de-Campos, Spong, and Chandraharan 2015; Bakker and van Geijn 2008; Reuwer, Bruinse, and Franx 2009), which are linked to neonatal mortality and morbidity. About 750,000 neonates die annually in India, more than anywhere else in the world. The decline in the neonatal mortality rate (NMR), from 52 per 1,000 live births in 1990 to 28 per 1,000 live births in 2013, has been slower than the reduction in mortality rates among infants and children under age five (Sankar and others 2016).

Preterm labor contributes to 43 percent of newborn deaths in India (Sankar and others 2016), a telling statistic that highlights the importance of maternal care close to and during labor. There is a dire need for timely obstetric care, especially in rural areas, which could be met by a simple, accurate, and time- and cost-efficient labor monitoring tool that can be used at the grassroots level, particularly at the estimated 150,000 subcenters manned by auxiliary nurse midwives (Garg, Singh, and Grover 2012).

Such a tool should be not only accurate but operationally seamless. The current procedure for recording fetal heartbeat and uterine contractions during pregnancy, cardiotocography (CTG), has serious challenges. First, the equipment is bulky, expensive, and difficult to use; it requires clinical expertise and cannot be scaled up in low-income settings with poor access to health care (see figure 1.1). Second, its performance is affected by maternal obesity and maternal movements. And third, it is more sensitive to changes during the second stage of labor, rather than in the more crucial first stage. Studies have found that the contraction rates and amplitudes measured by CTG were the same in term labor and nonlabor patients, which is a disadvantage, because the two types of patients have to be clinically distinguished (Bakker, Zikkenheimer, and van Geijn 2008; Garfield and Maner 2007; Vlemminx and others 2017). CTG also has poor ability to predict premature

FIGURE 1.1

Cardiotocography machine for labor monitoring

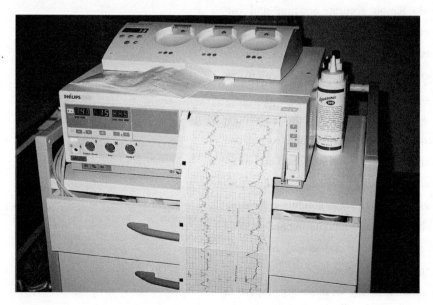

Photo: IndiaMart website. Cardiotocography machine fetal monitor.

labor and cannot aid in clinical decisions much in advance of complications (Iams 2003; Maner and others 2003; Maul, Saade, and Garfield 2005). Thus, a replacement for CTG is urgently needed for accuracy, feasible design, and efficiency in low-income settings.

SOLUTION

Our team has developed a novel solution for monitoring uterine contractions and fetal heart rate (FHR) to reduce neonatal morbidity and mortality. It consists of a Doppler-based fetal heart monitor, Fetosense, and an interconnected device for evaluating the pattern of uterine contractions, called U-Act (figures 1.2–1.4).

Fetosense is a smartphone-enabled, point-of-care FHR monitoring device to be used after 24 weeks of gestation. Our start-up developed it to be an indigenous alternative to CTG at a substantially lower price. Because the device is a point-of-care solution, all gynecologists and midwives can afford to make FHR monitoring available in their respective centers, and its portability will allow remote monitoring of multiple patients at a time.

Fetosense works on the principle of ultrasonic Doppler, which is a proven technology. Studies have shown that heart rate variability indexes significantly correlate with fetal distress (Jezewski, Wrobel, and Horoba 2006). Use of Fetosense will allow analysis of FHR trace (number of minutes), baseline FHR in beats per minute (bpm), tachycardia (mean FHR > 160 bpm), bradycardia (mean FHR < 110 bpm), accelerations, decelerations, beat-to-beat variability, and the three-tier FHR interpretation system.

U-Act is a smartphone-enabled, portable, battery-powered, and Bluetooth-operated point-of-care device to measure uterine electrical activity. The tool, which is based on the proven principle of electrohysterography, measures the electrical impulses in the uterine muscle that precede the mechanical contractions (Verdenik, Pajntar, and Leskošek 2001). U-Act targets the underlying cause of contractions and can provide an authentic picture of the internal

FIGURE 1.2

Fetosense: A smartphone-based tool for fetal heart rate monitoring

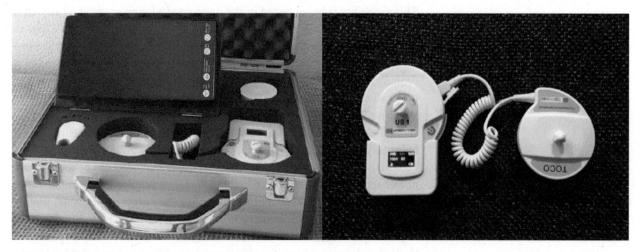

Fetosense costs half as much as a cardiotocography machine, is portable, gives real-time results, can be used anytime anywhere, provides positioning assistance for nonexperts, and enables remote monitoring and interpretation.

FIGURE 1.3

Field use of Fetosense by CareNx team

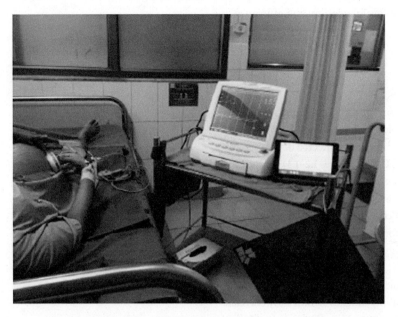

Photo: CareNX Innovations Private Limited, Mumbai, India.
Note: Side-by-side comparison of a CTG machine and Fetosense. Fetosense showed beat-to-beat variability in fetal heart rate comparable to the standard of care in 97 percent of cases, as cited in the validation certificate included in annex 1C.

uterine activity to guide clinical decisions. We are currently validating U-Act against the standard cardiotocography ("toco") in a hospital in Mumbai. U-Act may prove to be a better option because of reported problems of accuracy found in cardiotocography, the need for greater technical expertise, the cost, and the medical risks associated with another method—that is, the intra-uterine pressure catheterization (Mandile 2017; Rood 2012; Wilmink and others 2008). U-Act can record uterine contraction frequencies, amplitudes, and durations over 10-minute intervals. We developed U-Act to record uterine activity without being sensitive to maternal movements and obesity and without requiring maternal skin preparation (such as skin scraping). The filtered contraction signals can be transferred as data points directly to a smartphone for reporting results to doctors, to enable prompt clinical decision making (figure 1.4). In the ongoing validation study, U-Act will be able to provide the following results: sensitivity, specificity, positive and negative predictive value, false positive contraction ratio, false negative contraction ratio, and contraction consistency index.

Evidence from electrohysterography shows that U-Act can also be used to predict premature labor in women reporting with preterm contractions, based on analysis of uterine electrical activity (Verdenik, Pajntar, and Leskošek 2001). This is a crucial benefit, because current approaches for predicting premature labor (for example, cervical examination or assessment of biomarkers) are expensive. U-Act is a noninvasive, passive sensor that can provide comprehensive uterine contraction patterns and alert doctors to the likelihood of prematurity. This capability is being tested in the ongoing validation study at a hospital in Mumbai. We will compare actual birth outcomes with a predictive logistic regression model, to assess the sensitivity and specificity of U-Act in the prediction of premature labor. Predicting prematurity will enable the clinician to prolong the pregnancy using tocolytics and to provide steroids for fetal lung maturation to reduce neonatal morbidity, should a delivery occur before term. We also will calculate the Morbidity Assessment Index for Newborns, to understand if early prediction of prematurity has a positive effect on neonatal morbidity, as prior research has shown (Verma and others 2005).

Because Fetosense and U-Act are battery operated, they can be used in low-power settings. They also have low maintenance requirements, unlike bulky, power-consuming CTG machines. Together they offer an accurate, mobile, and efficient solution for reducing neonatal morbidity and mortality. Their use requires minimal technical skills, resulting in low-cost, scalable implementation in low-income settings for effective monitoring of maternal and fetal health during labor.

FIGURE 1.4

Highly portable components of U-Act

a. U-Act

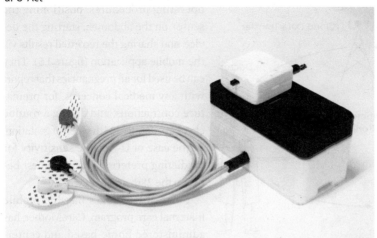

b. Processing unit

c. Surface electrode patch

d. Wireless module (BLE 4.0)

Photos: CareNX Innovations Private Limited, Mumbai, India.

FIGURE 1.5
Use of U-Act

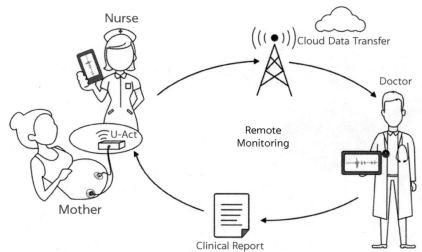

IMPLEMENTATION

Both Fetosense and U-Act employ simple operating procedures: positioning the sensor on the abdomen, starting the device, and sharing the recorded results via the mobile application (figure 1.5). They can be used for all pregnancies that report with any medical concerns, for premature contractions, and during a routine checkup after the 24th week of gestation. In the case of U-Act, the sensitivity for predicting preterm labor is highest between the 28th and 35th week.

Since 2015, India's flagship mobile maternal care program, CareMother, has administered home-based and center-based antenatal tests conducted by health workers, who use portable diagnostic kits and a smartphone app to share results via the cloud. Currently, 260 community health workers in 10 states of India and more than 15 implementing partners—a mix of nonprofits, private hospitals, and government agencies—are part of CareMother. These workers can be trained to use Fetosense and U-Act. CareMother is an existing vehicle for validation and further scale-up of these solutions. Since 2015, CareMother has registered 30,000 pregnancies and identified 12,000 high-risk pregnancies across the country.

We have also developed a separate mobile application for Fetosense and U-Act to report results to doctors already working in primary health centers under CareMother. We plan to offer the machines at $1,200–$1,500—far less than a standard cardiotocography machine, which costs $3,500–$4,500.

CASE STUDY: DEMONSTRATION OF PROOF OF CONCEPT

In October 2017, CareNX Innovations validated Fetosense against the standard of care, the cardiotocographapy, including through an assessment of fetal heart rate (nonstress test [NST]) and uterine contractions (toco). The study was conducted at Nanavati Super Speciality Hospital, in Mumbai, under the supervision of Dr. P. G. Natarajan, a world-renowned expert in NST interpretation with over 20 years of research and clinical experience. In the analysis of the first 50 of 100 samples, diversity was maintained according to statistical requirements by considering sample distribution over a gestational age range (24–40 weeks), maternal weight classes (48–102 kilograms), and maternal age (21–40 years), and samples met high-risk criteria (10 percent of mothers). For each sample, fetal heart rate (FHR) was recorded with cardiotocography and Fetosense, one after another, for a duration of 5–20 minutes each, plotted over a 1 centimeter/minute scale. Results verified by the specialist doctor were as follows:

- Interpretability: Excellent.

- Efficacy toward sample distribution: Good.

- Baseline FHR variation: Statistically insignificant difference in mean FHR, as measured by Fetosense and CTG (see figure 1.6 and table 1.1).

FIGURE 1.6

Baseline fetal heart rate as measured by standard nonstress test and Fetosense

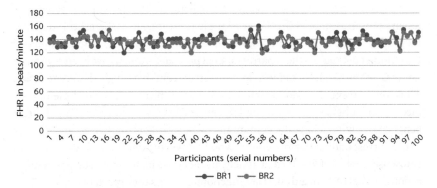

Source: Derived from data analysis after the CareNX Innovations validation study for Fetosense.

Note: BR1 = baseline fetal heart rate measured by standard nonstress test (NST) device; BR2 = baseline fetal heart rate measured by Fetosense; FHR = fetal heart rate.

Table 1.1 **Baseline fetal heart rate as measured by Fetosense and nonstress test**

	NONSTRESS TEST	FETOSENSE
Mean fetal heart rate*	138.7	136.8
Standard deviation	8.1	7.1
Range	120–160	120–155

Source: Summary of results of the CareNX Innovations validation study for Fetosense.

*p = 0.06974 (nonsignificant difference between the two sets of values).

- Usability: Fetosense has end-to-end wireless configuration, so it is easy to carry and set up, and printing graphs through a wireless A-4 printer is convenient.

- Maintenance: Fetosense can work for almost six hours when fully charged to perform almost 40 NST tests in a single charging cycle.

- Fetosense showed good beat-to-beat variability regardless of maternal age or gestational age.

U-Act, based on the method of electrohysterography (EHG), to assess uterine electrical activity, is currently being validated against cardiotocography at an urban hospital in Mumbai, with a sample of 100 pregnant women reporting with contractions from the 25th week onward. EHG is a proven technique to measure uterine electrical activity in the uterine muscle that leads to its constraction (Vlemminx and others 2017; Bakker, Zikkenheimer, and van Geijn 2008; Garfield and Maner 2007; Iams 2003; Maul, Saade, and Garfield 2005; Maner et al. 2003; Jezewski, Wrobel, and Horoba 2006; Verdenik, Pajntar, and Leskošek 2001.).

TARGET MARKET

Our solution for reducing neonatal morbidity and mortality will target pregnant mothers and fetuses in particular in parts of the world with poor access to antenatal and postnatal care. Once the current validation study of U-Act is completed, we will focus on selected intervention sites under CareMother, India's mobile maternal care program. To maximize diversity, we will select two urban sites (a hospital and a health post) and two rural sites (a primary health center and a subcenter) to implement the solution. CareMother works with a range of urban and rural partners; any grants that we receive will be used to build strategic collaborations with the current organizations at our selected sites. Building their capacity will be critical to scaling up our solutions. Two such partners will be selected—one catering to urban slums in Mumbai, the other working in rural areas in Maharashtra. Together they will provide access to the four intervention sites. According to the updated CareMother data across these partners, 4,153 pregnant women have been registered under CareMother; 1,647 of those women (40 percent) have high-risk pregnancies. Thus, the current CareMother intervention areas provide a strong base of low-income direct beneficiaries for implementing Fetosense and U-Act. The indirect beneficiaries will include the community health workers, midwives, and doctors at the corresponding health centers, who will be empowered with the validated Fetosense and U-Act for efficient, timely, and effective management of fetal complications. A total of 98 health staff are functioning across these partners.

SOCIAL IMPACT

In 2015, India reported 48.1 million pregnancies, of which 54 percent led to deliveries (Yadavar 2019). Current CareMother data show that 50–60 percent of these 26 million annual viable pregnancies are high risk and would benefit from monitoring, using Fetosense and U-Act. These pregnancies are served by an estimated 135,000 hospitals and more than 300,000 clinics in India. However, India has only 35,000 gynecologists. Fetosense and U-Act need to be used at each of the facilities so that nurses, midwives, and other clinicians can conduct these critical evaluations. The same applies for midwives at India's 150,000 subcenters. With greater use of the devices, the results can be interpreted automatically using machine-learning algorithms, and recurrent patterns in FHR and uterine activity can be correlated to fetal cardiac function, metabolic acidosis, and neonatal outcomes. This system will reduce the continuous dependence on doctors for managing high-risk cases and substantially increase the use of remote monitoring by doctors. Moreover, uterine activity patterns predicting premature labor will enable obstetric interventions such as steroid treatment for fetal lung maturation, given at an early stage to reduce birth asphyxia, and prolongation of pregnancy to term using tocolytic drugs, wherever possible. These devices can help save the lives of a significant number of the 3.5 million babies who are born preterm in India annually, who otherwise would die of complications or suffer short-term and long-term morbidities.

We will use the following impact indicators to measure success and to compare data from a comparison group, such as an adjacent CareMother intervention area receiving standard maternal care at labor and in the last two months of pregnancy. We expect a difference (effect size) between the two groups of at least 15–20 percent in the achievement of these indicators, as follows:

1. Reduction in neonatal mortality rates at study sites (assessed within 28 days of life)

2. Reduction in the incidence of neonatal asphyxia because of early detection of fetal distress by Fetosense and U-Act and the resulting improved antenatal and intrapartum management (assessed within 28 days of life)

3. Reduction in the incidence of infant developmental delay (assessed periodically within the first year of life)

4. Improvement in feeding behaviors and breastfeeding rate and quality (assessed during the first six months of life)

5. Improved infant cognitive and behavioral indicators at one year using standardized assessments.

Indicators 3, 4, and 5 are based on the premise that prematurity leads to long-term morbidities. Early identification and prediction of premature labor through U-Act, and effective labor monitoring through Fetosense and U-Act, will lead the clinician to attempt to prolong the pregnancy (for example, by administration of tocolytic drugs) or provide appropriate obstetric intervention (for example, providing steroids for fetal lung maturation) to reduce newborn morbidity (commonly from asphyxia) and improve short-term and long-term infant health and developmental outcomes.

FINANCIAL SUSTAINABILITY

Revenue Model for Fetosense and U-Act

- Business-to-business (B2B): Government and developmental organizations

  CareNX Innovations will target government and developmental organizations for large sales with the initial pilot for Fetosense and U-Act. The team has experience piloting Fetosense in an urban private hospital (refer to proof of certification in annex 1C). The B2B model will involve direct sales of devices and an annual contract for software maintenance and updating. We also plan to experiment with a service model, in which CareNX is paid for every test performed and there is no capital investment. This model can be implemented through nongovernmental organization champions who work or wish to work with the government. It can increase the scalability of the solution.

- B2B/Business-to-business-to-consumer (B2B2C) in private hospitals

  Fetosense and U-Act will be offered to private hospitals on a subscription basis. There will be fees for enrolling in the system and recurring costs on a monthly basis, which will also include maintenance and software. We do not plan to position our system only as a fetal heart rate diagnosis device or a labor monitoring tool but more as a solution for fetal well-being, and we expect to extend additional services. For example, the results obtained via Fetosense and U-Act can be auto-interpreted and a prediction algorithm developed to correlate them with neonatal outcomes. This solution can link midwives, doctors, and gynecologists in low-resource settings with doctors and gynecologists in the urban segment or with medical experts for additional online (and remote) consultation.

- Business-to-consumer (B2C): Direct engagement with pregnant women

  Because Fetosense and U-Act are portable, wireless smartphone–connected devices, we might make them available through an appropriate market channel to engage pregnant women directly and offer them consultation by allowing them to select a doctor.

Existing financial support, such as from the CISCO Global Problem Solver Fund and Grand Challenges Canada, will help execute the commercial pilot of Fetosense and U-Act.

SCALABILITY

In addition to the points mentioned under "Social Impact," we plan to achieve scalability through the following growth model. We want to present and market the solution differently in the private versus public and urban versus rural health segments. In the private sector, we want to enable monitoring of high-risk mothers, both in clinics and remotely supervised by gynecologists. First, we will collaborate with the most influential urban gynecologists and promote the solution through local gynecology chapters and conferences. Meanwhile, we have forged an association with the Federation of Obstetrical and Gynaecological Societies in India (FOGSI), which includes 35,000 gynecologists. FOGSI "launched" Fetosense in June 2019, during its conference on obstetrics and gynecology in Hyderabad, India. Auto-interpretation of data will provide more objective and frequent results for remote monitoring. In the rural segment, where there is an acute scarcity of gynecologists, we will enable physicians to conduct nonstress testing and monitoring of uterine contractions. The system's auto-interpretation of data and the grade of severity flagged by the prediction algorithm will reduce dependence on the doctor. We can also extend fetal monitoring services through ground-level health workers, to enable nonstress testing at home or at nearby subcenters, during CareMother home visits, allowing patients with any anomalies to be promptly referred to secondary or tertiary facilities.

Our solution also aligns with the objectives of the government of India's Pradhan Mantri Surakshit Matritva Abhiyan (PMSMA). When used at a facility, it can increase the rate of institutional deliveries, a key objective of the government's National Health Mission to reduce maternal and neonatal mortality.

COMPETITOR ANALYSIS

Table 1.2 summarizes the competitor analysis with regard to Fetosense and U-Act. CareNX is the only market player to provide doorstep care with early-stage

TABLE 1.2 **Analysis of competitors**

CARENX AND COMPETITORS	NUMBER OF PARAMETER TESTS	DOORSTEP DIAGNOSTIC CARE	REFERRAL LINKS	EARLY HIGH-RISK IDENTIFICATION	NONSTRESS FETAL HEART RATE TEST	PRICE
CareNx	More than 8 prenatal tests and nonstress test	Yes	Yes	Yes	Yes	CareMother Kit: $400; Fetosense + U-Act: $1,200–$1,500
HealthCube	33 tests with vitals and diagnostics	Yes	Yes	No	No	$936
Janitri	Labor monitoring device	No	No	No	Yes	$1,000–$2,000
brün	Fetal heart rate and contraction	No	Yes	Yes	Yes	$2,000
Sattva Medtech	Fetal heart rate and contraction	No	No	No	Yes	$2,000
Monica Healthcare Ltd	Labor monitoring	No	No	Yes	Yes	$2,000
Dimagi	15 tests with vitals and diagnostics	Yes	Yes	No	No	Not available

diagnostics at an affordable price (through CareMother, a flagship program that operates in 10 Indian states).

ASSUMPTIONS, COST ANALYSIS, AND INCOME PROJECTION FOR THE NEXT THREE YEARS

See annexes 1E and 1F for the B2B assumptions and cost analysis, with a focus on the Fetosense component of the solution (which has been validated).

CHALLENGES AND MITIGATIONS

Market

Establishing a supply chain or distribution is a challenge for new health care devices. We will tackle it by partnering with organizations working with government health agencies. Our partner and implementing organizations under CareMother are closely connected with supply chain systems for other materials, such as essential medicines, point-of-care devices, and hospital supplies. We will also partner with pharmaceutical companies.

Operational

Ground-level operational challenges include staff training and retraining needs, field queries, and circumstances in which staff may have to tackle situations independently. With a comprehensive bilingual user manual, effective training, dedicated monitoring by a central team, and centralized helpline number, staff will be able to achieve their targets and resolve contingencies. For challenges arising from new test configurations, the software will be remotely upgraded on smartphones. Self-calibration of the devices will help, as will our continual effort to improve devices' accuracy (by performing back-end analytics).

Financial

No direct financial risk to the company (CareNX Innovations) is associated with these projects. The devices and software are comprehensive for maternal and child health needs during the perinatal period for the objectives this solution aims to achieve, and nearly all costs are linked only to the devices. Budgets for customers are clearly defined; with the funds provided, the implementation will be feasible and streamlined. The costs of procurement and development and recurring material costs were studied and tested during the baseline and prior field validations.

Regulatory

India's Central Drugs Standard Control Organization (CDSCO) guidelines mandate the physical and metrological standardizations necessary for demonstrating the safety and efficacy of a medical device before it can be marketed and used in India. This has been done for Fetosense by comparing its output with a previously approved device of a similar type (a standard nonstress test). U-Act is currently being validated against cardiotocography in an urban hospital. Any additional third-party validations will be obtained from authorized agencies or institutions at the field level.

We will also stay updated with any new regulations and meet the requirements with our strong in-house team, particularly given our experience with the CareMother program.

ANNEX 1A. LINKS TO ARTICLES THAT DEMONSTRATE RECOGNITION OF CAREMOTHER IN THE MEDIA

1. *Your Story*
   Mannan, L. 2017. "CareNX Innovations Takes Quality Healthcare to the Doorsteps of Rural Pregnant Women." *Your Story*, August 13. https://yourstory.com/2017/08/carenx-innovations-portable-pregnancy-care-villages/.

2. *Better India*
   Raja, V. 2018. "Thanks to This App, 3000 High Risk Pregnancies in Rural India Got Much-Needed Help!" *Better India*, May 18. https://www.thebetterindia.com/141847/high-risk-pregnancies-get-help-with-caremother-app/.

3. *Contemporary Ob/Gyn*
   Kronemyer, B. 2018. "Female Health Technology Takes Center Stage." *Contemporary Ob/Gyn*, October 22. http://www.contemporaryobgyn.net/technology/female-health-technology-takes-center-stage.

4. *Mumbai Mirror*
   Vaswani, A. 2018. "Three Social Entrepreneurs Felicitated by British Queen at Buckingham Palace in Final Year of Young Leaders Awards Programme." *Mumbai Mirror*, July 8. https://mumbaimirror.indiatimes.com/mumbai/other/city-change-makers-honoured-in-uk/articleshow/64901919.cms.

5. New Delhi Television Network
   Indo-Asian News Service. 2018. "Goggle Launchpd Accelerator India Shortlists 10 Startups." *Gadgets 360*, New Delhi Television Network, August 31. https://gadgets.ndtv.com/apps/news/google- launchpad-accelerator-india-shortlists-10-startups-1909076.

6. *TechCircle*
   Sharma, S. 2018. "Meet the 16 Winners of Govt-Backed Innovation Programme IIGP [India Innovation Growth Programme]." *TechCircle*, August 3. https://techcircle.vccircle.com/2018/08/03/meet-the-16-winners-of-govt-backed-innovation-programme-iigp/.

7. *Forbes*
   Thorpe, D. 2016. "14 Noteworthy Social Ventures Looking to Scale." *Forbes*, August 22. https://www.forbes.com/sites/devinthorpe/2016/08/22/14-noteworthy-social-ventures-looking-to-scale/#2abfec1b4b01.

ANNEX 1B. LINKS TO VIDEOS OF PRESENTATIONS RELATED TO CAREMOTHER

1. CareMother mJoy Pregnancy: https://youtu.be/kFnaeSplc5s.

2. Adopt a Mother (Mission): https://www.youtube.com/watch?v=UXR7xedrh_w.

3. World Health Summit: https://youtu.be/aNvYK2wRUQI.

4. The Miller Centre for Social Entrepreneurship: https://youtu.be/9KbLSwJUptI.

ANNEX 1C. CERTIFICATE OF VALIDATION OF FETOSENSE BY AN URBAN HOSPITAL

FIGURE 1C
Certificate of validation

To

Date: 09th January 2018

CareNX Innovations Pvt. Ltd.
IIT Bombay, Powai, Mumbai- 400076

SUBJECT: Results from the validation study of a smartphone based Non Stress Test (NST) monitor

BACKGROUND
CareNX Innovations Pvt. Ltd., from IIT Bombay has developed a smartphone based fetal heart rate (FHR) monitor (called FETON) to perform non-stress test (NST). CareNX had been granted a permission by Nanavati Super Speciality Hospital on 14th of October 2017 to perform a comparative validation study of FETON against standard of care NST device (i.e a CTG machine) for 100 samples. This study is being conducted under the supervision of Dr. P. G. Natarajan from Nanavati who is a world renowned expert for NST interpretation with over 20 years of practical & research experience.

OBJECTIVE
This letter highlights the comparative analysis done over first 50 samples obtained. Key areas for comparison include interpretability, efficacy, ease-of-use and performance. This letter also outlines personal opinions of Dr. Natrajan while using FETON for the period of last 80 days.

PROCEDURE AND REQUIREMENTS
CareNX's representative has provided operational and technical support for FETON setup. The diversity of first 50 samples is maintained as per the statistical requirements by considering it's distribution among gestational age (24-40 weeks), weight classes (48-102 kg), age (21-40 years) and high risk criteria (10%). For each sample, FHR has been recorded one after another from NST machine and FETON device respectively; for the duration of 5-20 minutes each; plotted over 1 cm/minute scale. Graphs obtained from both instruments are kept together for Dr. Natrajan to interpret both at the same time.

OUTCOMES
- Interpretability:- Excellent
- Efficacy towards sample distributions:- Good
- Baseline FHR:- There is a variation of ~5bpm c̄ FETON but NST is dependent on variations and not absolute values except at extremes (< 110 + >160)
- Beat-by-beat variability:- FETON BETTER FOR INTERPRETATION
- Usability & robustness:- FETON comes with end-to-end wireless configuration. Hence it was convenient to carry, move & setup the instrument. Printing graphs through wireless A4 printer was easy. Robust device quality and easy configuration made it handy.
- Battery performance:- FETON can work for almost 6 hours once it is fully charged. This is quite sufficient time to perform almost 40 NST tests in single charging cycle.

DISCLAIMER
The purpose of the study with FETON is strictly for the validation purpose. The interpretation from FETON graphs were not used for making any clinical decisions for the samples under consideration.

Dr. P. G. Natarajan

Dr. P.G. Natrajan, MD FRCOG   MMC 27447
Dept. Prenatal Medicine, NANAVATI HOSPITAL,
S. V. Road, Vile Parle West,   Mumbai-400056.
Tel.: 02226118000 e mail: natkingpg@gmail.com

ANNEX 1D. PATENT (E-FILING) FOR FETOSENSE

FIGURE 1D
Patent (e-filing)

INTELLECTUAL
PROPERTY **INDIA**
PATENTS|DESIGNS |TRADE MARKS
GEOGRAPHICAL INDICATIONS

Controller General of Patents, Designs & Trade
Marks
S.M.Road,Antop Hill, Mumbal-400037
Tel No. (091)(022) 241377010,24141026 Fax No. 022
24130387
E-mall: mumbal-patent@nic.in
Web Site: www.ipindia.gov.in

G.A.R.6
[See Rule 22(1)]
RECEIPT

Docket No 33204

Date/Time 2018/07/26 13:07:51

To
USHA ATHREYA CHANDRASEKHAR

UserId: usha

3E1, Court Chambers, 3rd Floor, 35, New
Marine Lines Road,

CBR Detail:

Sr. No.	Ref. No./Application No.	App. Number	Amount Paid	C.B.R. No.	Form Name	Remarks
1	E-106/503/2018/MUM	201821028090	0	----	FORM28	
2	201821028090	TEMP/E-1/29553/2018-MUM	1600	14082	FORM 1	Optimization and Localization of Pulsating Signals

TransactionID	Payment Mode	Challan Identification Number	Amount Paid	Head of A/C No
N-0000398242	Online Bank Transfer	02806342607201850294	1600.00	1475001020000001

Total Amount : ₹ 1600
Amount in Words: Rupees One Thousand Six Hundred Only

Received from USHA ATHREYA CHANDRASEKHAR the sum of ₹ 1600 on account of Payment of fee for above
mentioned Application/Forms.

* This is a computer generated receipt, hecnce no signature required.

Print

ANNEX 1E. FETOSENSE BUSINESS-TO-BUSINESS ASSUMPTIONS

TABLE 1E **Fetosense business-to-business assumptions**

USAGE	Fixed price model
Number of tests per doctor per year	640
Average number of mothers per year	400
Average number of tests per normal mother	1
Average numbers of tests per high-risk mother	4
Average high-risk patients (%)	20

(continued)

TABLE 1E, *continued*

HARDWARE	Amount
Fetosense kit cost (US$)	**560**
Probe	300
Movement marker	3
Charger	2
Straps	15
Speaker	15
Bag, etc.	75
Tab	150
Hardware replacement period (years)	
Probe	5
Movement marker	1
Tab	2
Straps	2
Hardware replacement cost (average years)	**71**
Probe	60
Movement marker	3
Straps	7.5

SOFTWARE (variable costs)	Amount
New data storage cost per test per year	**1**
Data storage cost per test per year (US$)	1
Years of data storage required per patient	1

SERVICE	Amount
Customer onboarding cost	**23**
Days required from CareNx per onboard	50%
Onboarding member per day cost	20
Travel cost per meeting (roundtrip)	3
Tech support inquiries per year	**4**
Average inquiries per user	4

(continued)

TABLE 1E, *continued*

Cost per inquiry	5
Days required from CareNX tech support per inquiry	0.25
Daily cost of tech support member (US$)	20
Hardware replacement service cost per year (US$)	**6**
Trips per year	1
Average travel cost per trip (roundtrip)	6

MARKETING OVERHEAD (fixed cost)	Amount
Marketing cost per month	**800**
Number of meetings per month	100
Number of meetings per lead (variable)	5
Sales person cost per month (US$)	600
Travel cost per meeting (US$)	2
Travel cost per month (US$)	200
Marketing cost per customer	**267**
Number of leads met per month per sales person (capacity)	20
Conversion rate of lead to customer (%)	15
Number of customers per month per sales person	3

OTHER FIXED COSTS	Amount
Finance and administration HR cost per year (US$)	**1,440**
Finance and administration per month (US$)	600
Finance and administration time allocated for B2B (%)	20
Software maintenance and upgrade team cost per year (US$)	**15,000**
HQ-level marketing and branding of Fetosense per year (US$)	**1,600**
Website cost per year (US$)	100
Marketing/branding person salary per month (US$)	500
Marketing/branding person time allocated to Fetosense B2B (%)	25

Note: B2B = business to business; HR = human resources; HQ = headquarters.

ANNEX 1F. COST ANALYSIS

TABLE 1F **Cost analysis**

TYPE OF COST	NUMBER OF DOCTORS (1 KIT = 1 DOCTOR)
1. Acquisition and activation	290
Customer onboarding cost	23
Marketing cost per customer	267
2. Start-up costs (variable by number of kits sold)	560
Fetosense kit cost	560
3. Annual costs per kit	772
Hardware replacement cost (average per year)	112
New data storage cost per customer-account	640
Cost of tech support inquiries	20
4. Annual administration costs	18,040

REFERENCES

Ayres-de-Campos, D., C. Y. Spong, and E. Chandraharan. 2015. "FIGO Consensus Guidelines on Intrapartum Fetal Monitoring: Cardiotocography." *International Journal of Gynecology and Obstetrics* 131 (1): 13–24.

Bakker, P. C., and H. P. van Geijn. 2008. "Uterine Activity: Implications for the Condition of the Fetus." *Journal of Perinatal Medicine* 36 (1): 30–37.

Bakker, P. C., M. Zikkenheimer, and H. P. van Geijn. 2008. "The Quality of Intrapartum Uterine Activity Monitoring. *Journal of Perinatal Medicine* 36 (3): 197–201.

Garfield, R. E., and W. L. Maner. 2007. "Physiology and Electrical Activity of Uterine Contractions." *Seminars in Cell and Developmental Biology* 18 (3): 289–95.

Garg, S., R. Singh, and M. Grover. 2012. "India's Health Workforce: Current Status and the Way Forward." *National Medical Journal of India* 25 (2): 111.

Iams, J. D. 2003. "Prediction and Early Detection of Preterm Labor." *Obstetrics and Gynecology* 101 (2): 402–12.

Jezewski, J., J. Wrobel, and K. Horoba. 2006. "Comparison of Doppler Ultrasound and Direct Electrocardiography Acquisition Techniques for Quantification of Fetal Heart Rate Variability." *IEEE Transactions on Biomedical Engineering* 53 (5): 855–64.

Maner, W. L., R. E. Garfield, H. Maul, G. Olson, and G. Saade. 2003. "Predicting Term and Preterm Delivery with Transabdominal Uterine Electromyography." *Obstetrics and Gynecology* 101 (6): 1254–60.

Mandile, O. 2017. "Intrauterine Pressure Catheter." *Embryo Project Encyclopedia,* July 18.

Maul, H., G. Saade, and R. E. Garfield. 2005. "Prediction of Term and Preterm Parturition and Treatment Monitoring by Measurement of Cervical Cross-Linked Collagen Using Light-Induced Fluorescence." *Acta obstetricia et gynecologica Scandinavica* 84 (6): 534–36.

Reuwer, P., H. Bruinse, and A. Franx. 2009. *Proactive Support of Labor: The Challenge of Normal Childbirth.* Cambridge, U.K.: Cambridge University Press.

Rood, K. M. 2012. "Complications Associated with Insertion of Intrauterine Pressure Catheters: An Unusual Case of Uterine Hypertonicity and Uterine Perforation Resulting in Fetal Distress after Insertion of an Intrauterine Pressure Catheter." *Case Reports in Obstetrics and Gynecology* 2012: 517461. doi:10.1155/2012/517461.

Sankar, M. J., S. B. Neogi, J. Sharma, M. J. Chauhan, R. Srivastava, P. K. Prabhakar, A. Khera, R. Kumar, S. Zodpey, and V. K. Paul. 2016. "State of Newborn Health in India." *Journal of Perinatology* 36: S3.

Verdenik, I., M. Pajntar, and B. Leskošek. 2001. "Uterine Electrical Activity as Predictor of Preterm Birth in Women with Preterm Contractions." *European Journal of Obstetrics and Gynecology and Reproductive Biology* 95 (2): 149–53.

Verma, A., A. Weir, J. Drummond, and B. F. Mitchell. 2005. "Performance Profile of an Outcome Measure: Morbidity Assessment Index for Newborns." *Journal of Epidemiology and Community Health.* 59 (5): 420–26.

Vlemminx, M. W., K. M. Thijssen, G. I. Bajlekov, J. P. Dieleman, M. B. Van Der Hout-Van Der Jagt, and S. Guid Oei. 2017. "Electrohysterography for Uterine Monitoring during Term Labour Compared to External Tocodynamometry and Intra-uterine Pressure Catheter." *European Journal of Obstetrics and Gynecology and Reproductive Biology* 215: 197–205.

Wilmink, F. A., F. F. Wilms, R. Heydanus, B. W. Mol, and D. N. Papatsonis. 2008. "Fetal Complications after Placement of an Intrauterine Pressure Catheter: A Report of Two Cases and Review of the Literature. *Journal of Maternal–Fetal and Neonatal Medicine* 21 (12): 880–83.

Yadavar, S. 2019. "Almost Half of Pregnancies in India Were Mistimed or Unwanted." *Fact Checker,* December 18. https://factchecker.in/almost-half-of-pregnancies-in-india-were-mistimed-or-unwanted/.

2 Using Location Intelligence to Solve the Urban Sanitation Crisis

JOHN PETER ARCHER, *Cofounder and partnerships director*

LINDSEY NOAKES, *Cofounder and programmes director*

LUIZ HENRIQUE RODRIGUES, *Data analyst*

FIONA WATTERS, *Research assistant*

ABSTRACT Gather uses location data intelligence to get toilets to people who need them. We use geospatial analysis to inform investment in sanitation infrastructure and services to prevent fecal contamination of water supplies in high-risk areas. Our innovation empowers municipal governments to preempt repetitive outbreaks of enteric and diarrheal disease.

By 2025, we want to transform how sanitation is provided for 5 million people across four emerging cities. We will do so through three complementary programs:

1. Our local sanitation data hubs bring together key sanitation providers across cities to transform how they share data and act on analysis.

2. Our global Sanitation Data Commission leverages the work of the hubs to create data standards for urban sanitation.

3. Thought leadership provides transparent, trusted evidence to advance the conversation around data for development.

Gather focuses on helping implement action that will achieve Sustainable Development Goal (SDG) 6.2 (universal access to adequate and equitable sanitation). We are starting in Antananarivo, the capital of Madagascar. We are working in the 5th arrondissement, home to around 350,000 people, with plans to expand to the rest of the city and then into Lusaka in Zambia, Nakuru in Kenya, and Kumasi in Ghana.

Cross-sector collaboration is central to our approach. As a result, we are also playing our part toward achieving SDGs 3.3 (end waterborne diseases), 6.1 (achieve universal access to drinking water), 11.6 (reduce adverse environmental impact of cities), and 17.6 (enhance knowledge sharing for innovation).

Team Gather, London, United Kingdom.

PROBLEM AND CONTEXT

Currently, 2.5 billion people around the world live in cities without access to a safe, clean toilet. Without toilets, cities cannot thrive. Water sources get dangerously polluted by fecal waste, children get sick, and household members cannot work. Without toilets, girls drop out of school when they start to menstruate. According to the Bill & Melinda Gates Foundation, every year the urban sanitation crisis results in increased health care costs, decreased income, and reduced productivity, totaling more than US$200 billion (Belton 2018).

We started investigating the key drivers of the urban sanitation crisis in 2016. We focused on why there has been no change in the number of people living in cities who do not have access to a proper toilet since 1990 (the figure has stayed at around 2.5 billion for the past three decades). As part of our research, we connected with more than 100 sanitation organizations that are working to tackle the global crisis.

We found that a lack of accurate, actionable data was hindering their efforts to get sanitation to those who need it most. Sanitation organizations collect data as part of their operations, but these data are often of poor quality and are rarely shared or analyzed fully to produce actionable insight. Sanitation organizations are working hard to tackle the urban sanitation crisis, but without proper data they do not know where their services are most needed.

The global sector collects a lot of data, but different entities do not record the location, type of toilet, or amount of waste in the same way. As a result, no one can curate data from a variety of sources to visualize the true state of sanitation in a city. Without accurate geolocation, we cannot gain additional insight from data sets on demographics, topography, and flood risk, all of which are critical to providing high-quality sanitation services. Without this enhancement, sanitation providers miss out on key insights they need for service design and expansion.

The lack of data interoperability across the sector has also led to costly duplication of effort. Too often, the same areas have been surveyed and the same low-quality data have been collected repeatedly in slightly different ways. This approach is unsustainable and wasteful, in a sector with limited resources. The resulting data gap is preventing the entire sanitation sector from getting toilets to people who need them most.

Our research was corroborated by the World Bank Group (2017), which reported that a lack of trusted, actionable data had led to an ineffective allocation of resources across the sanitation sector. In 2018, the United Nations found that the lack of high-quality data had limited the sector's ability to monitor its progress and stated that "reliable, consistent and, whenever possible, disaggregated data are essential to stimulate political commitment, inform policy making and decision making" (UN-Water 2018, 17).

We need better data, particularly given that the urban sanitation crisis disproportionately disadvantages the most vulnerable people in society. Children, women, gender minorities, the elderly, and differently abled people are severely affected by a limited or complete lack of safe, clean, accessible toilets. Yet they are most often ignored during data collection and least able to advocate for their needs to decision makers. They remain invisible: If you are not counted, you don't count. Data underpin accountability, transparency, and participation; they are critical to ensure that sanitation providers can get toilets to those who need them most.

SOLUTION

Approach

Location data matter. In previous initiatives, we trained young people to map household sanitation for 180,000 people in Nairobi, Kenya; launched a demo of an online global platform for data sharing; and hosted the world's first data dive for urban sanitation, which assessed sanitation services for 370,000 people in Lusaka, Zambia.

We are now focused on demonstrating how enhanced geospatial analysis can help municipal decision makers preempt outbreaks of enteric and diarrheal diseases (for example, cholera) by directing their investments into sanitation infrastructure and services in high-risk areas. International policy makers have frequently used precision mapping to understand the causality of outbreaks in enteric and diarrheal diseases. This descriptive analysis is helpful for historical cases but has rarely been used for predicting and preventing future outbreaks.

We have three principles of action (see figure 2.1):

1. Municipal governments and their partners lack the capacity to conduct predictive analysis. We reduce this data burden and provide them with the critical analytical capacity they need via a simple, easy-to-use dashboard.

2. We can generate enhanced geospatial health data sets by linking them to data on sanitation service provision and contextual data sets, including demographics, topography, and flooding risk. This insight underpins accountability, collaboration, and action.

3. We can inform better decision making on investments and help prevent repetitive diarrheal disease outbreaks in low-income communities by providing predictive insight on where disease outbreaks will occur.

Pioneering the geospatial sanitation flow diagram

A key component of our work is the creation of geospatial sanitation flow diagrams (SFDs). Traditional SFDs, a Bill & Melinda Gates Foundation–backed initiative, show where fecal waste enters the environment and pollutes groundwater and rivers along the sanitation value chain. The tool is two dimensional and is undertaken as a one-off exercise. By transforming local data practices (including the standardization, collection, management, sharing, and analysis of data), we are transforming the SFD into a

FIGURE 2.1

Gather's method of standardized data collection and geospatial analysis for informed decision making

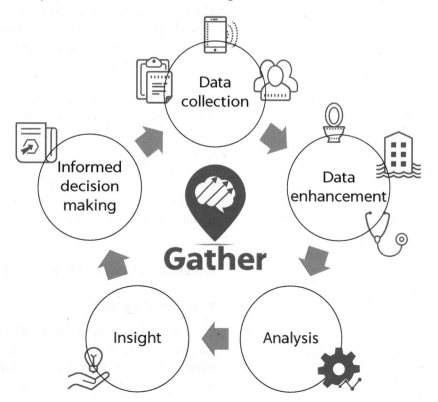

FIGURE 2.2

Turning location data into insight using geospatial visualizations in Lusaka, Zambia

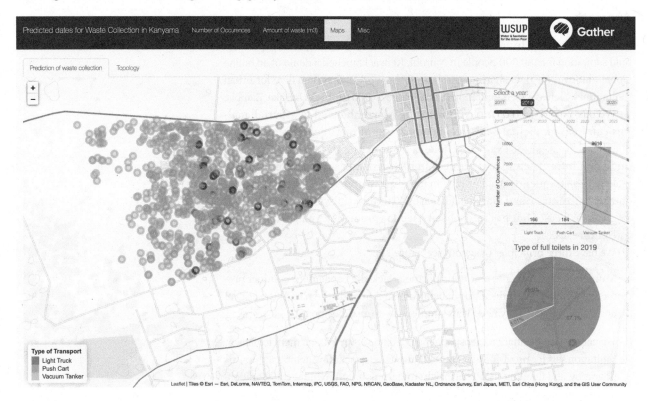

"live" visualization that indicates where investment and action are needed within a geographic area.

For the first time, decision makers will be able to understand whether the problem of fecal waste is, for example, that a lack of toilets is forcing people to defecate outside or that companies are dumping the fecal waste into rivers because there are not enough transfer or treatment stations. Our geospatial SFDs will enable government, private, and nonprofit sanitation organizations to work together to target and monitor their projects effectively to prevent fecal waste from entering water sources. For example, figure 2.2 shows the geospatial visualization in the informal settlement of Kanyama, in Lusaka, the capital of Zambia. The geospatial visualization predicts when on-site sanitation units will need to be emptied. This analysis is key for creating a geospatial SFD.

The users of the geospatial SFDs will be decision makers seeking to expand sanitation services for disadvantaged or low-income communities in emerging cities around the world. They include municipal governments, policy makers, sanitation providers, and large-scale investors and donors.

IMPLEMENTATION AND APPLICATION

Sanitation data hubs

The success of the geospatial SFD will be measured not by its predictive analysis but also by whether it leads to action. That is why the world's first geospatial SFD will be a collaborative effort with decision makers from Antananarivo, the capital of Madagascar. Together, we are launching a sanitation data hub that will transform how local decision makers collect, share, and act on their data. The hub's activities, successes, and challenges will help create a playbook to inform how we scale the hub's activities throughout Antananarivo and replicate hubs in other emerging cities (see figure 2.3).

Gather is launching its hubs in Antananarivo because Madagascar is rated fourth worst in the world for sanitation provision. In Antananarivo, 67 percent of people use unimproved pit latrines, 7 percent use bucket toilets, and 4 percent are without any toilet at all. The vast majority of the urban poor live in high-density, flood-prone neighborhoods. Antananarivo is growing at around 5 percent per year, increasing pressure on already limited services. Diarrheal diseases are the second leading cause of death after malaria and affect more than half of children under the age of five. In Antananarivo, 82 percent of the population does not have access to proper sanitation (WHO and UNICEF JMP 2015), and most fecal waste that is collected is dumped either into the Ikopa River or around the city (Artelia Madagascar 2014).

The water, sanitation, and hygiene (WASH) ministry's Suivi Eau et Assainissement à Madagascar database does not contain data on sanitation infrastructure in urban areas. Data published by the water and sanitation sector's global Joint Monitoring Programme lack geospatial information on waste collection and processing. This data gap makes it difficult for Antananarivo authorities to build a case for vital investment in on-site sanitation and treatment infrastructure.

To launch the hub, we have brought together the municipal government, utility company, and key private and nonprofit sanitation providers from Antananarivo:

- The Commune Urbaine d'Antananarivo, which is responsible for developing a water and sanitation strategy for the city of Antananarivo. The city of Antananarivo is divided into six administrative arrondissements. The 5th arrondissement will be the focus of this project.

- The Service Autonome de Maintenance de la Ville d'Antananarivo (SAMVA), which is responsible for sanitation service provision and waste collection in Antananarivo.

- Loowatt Madagascar, which delivers household sanitation using high-quality waterless flush toilet and sanitation solutions. Loowatt has been an active service provider in Antananarivo since 2011 and is preparing to grow its customer base to reach 3,000 households by 2021.

FIGURE 2.3

Locations of Gather's four proposed sanitation data hubs

- Water and Sanitation for the Urban Poor (WSUP), which is a trisector partnership between the private sector, civil society, and academia. WSUP's projects help transform cities to benefit millions of people, primarily from low-income communities, who lack access to water and sanitation. WSUP has conducted citywide surveys in eight cities across the world to assess the state of sanitation.

In its first year, the Antananarivo hub will start to improve the lives of 350,000 people by first transforming the local sanitation sector's decision-making process. For the first time, sanitation organizations will be able to do the following:

- Better understand the state of sanitation in the 5th arrondissement,

- Track progress in achieving SDG 6.2 (sanitation for all),

- Advocate for and direct investment to improving and expanding sanitation services.

Sanitation Data Commission

To complement the hubs, we are launching the Sanitation Data Commission. The commission will support the work of the hubs by setting a global data standard for urban sanitation data.

Users of the Sanitation Data Commission's data standard will be any organization seeking to collect, share, and understand sanitation data, including local sanitation organizations, national policy makers, and international regulators. The data standard will focus on the location of infrastructure, the volume of waste, and the transportation of waste. The creation of a data standard is our pathway to operating at a global scale. It will allow sanitation organizations across the world to collect, share, and curate data in a way that is currently impossible. By transforming global data practices, we can help maximize the impact of local efforts by turning insight into collaborative action.

We are appointing 10 commissioners from a diverse range of backgrounds and experiences. The commission's recommendations will be published online. Sanitation organizations from around the world will be invited to participate in a global survey of data practices, and early adopters will be encouraged to implement and test the new data standard.

The commission is part of Gather's opportunity to contribute to the conversation about using data for development. We are members of the Global Partnership for Sustainable Development Data; the work of our commission will be shared with the Collaborative on SDG Data Interoperability.

SCALE

Uptake is key to scale and will be driven by alignment with local priorities, user incentives, and financial sustainability.

Alignment with local priorities

Our work is aligned to the national and municipal governments' priorities for sanitation and public health. For example, one of the aims of the Madagascar government's Integrated Sanitation and Drainage Master Plan for Antananarivo is to better define and prioritize investment needs for the sanitation sector. This priority requires geospatial data of higher resolution than is currently available. Although the WASH ministry's existing database, Suivi Eau et Assainissement à Madagascar, hosts data on sanitation infrastructure, it still lacks data from urban areas.

Incentives

The geospatial SFD will create an accurate mechanism for sanitation organizations in Antananarivo to rigorously show where investable, sustainable sanitation services should be deployed. The mechanism will empower them to raise investment from financial instruments created to improve sanitation for the urban poor. The ongoing upload of data to the geospatial SFD through the activities of the sanitation data hubs will allow investors to track progress and measure the risk of their investment. Together, these elements will allow for the better allocation of resources and maintain an incentive for the standardization of data and the use of Gather's unique analysis.

Financial sustainability

Our work is currently supported by private philanthropists. Our sanitation data hub in Antananarivo has received support from the World Bank's Data Innovation Fund and the U.K. Department for International Development.

We forecast that our work can be funded through grants until at least the end of 2021. Between now and then, we want to move from a grants-based model to a partnership model. We want our data standard and analysis to become the benchmark through which the majority of global funders of sanitation assess the need within a city and track the long-term impact of their investments. We expect this model to be subscription based, keeping access to the insights free for local municipalities and city organizations.

We are also working with a team of pro bono analysts from Pricewaterhouse-Coopers (PwC) to identify additional sources of sustainable revenue that can fund our systems change work. They are exploring and forecasting options that include expert consulting, specialist services, thought leadership, and the partner subscription model outlined above.

COMPETITION

We consulted extensively as part of the design process for the sanitation data hub and the Sanitation Data Commission to ensure that no other similar initiatives are happening. No organization has created a global standard for urban sanitation data or proposed a methodology for cross-sector data collaboration at the municipal level.

Our work builds on lessons learned by similar initiatives for water data. The Joint Monitoring Programme (JMP) has established international definitions for the provision of water and sanitation services, and the Water Point Data Exchange (WPDx) has created a global standard for the collection, sharing, and use of rural water point data. Several excellent tools for data collection exist. One tool, mWater, lists a data standard for water points in its library. We are in conversation with the mWater team to list our data standard for urban sanitation, so that mWater users can easily adhere to it.

We are also positioning ourselves as a thought leader, sharing both successes and challenges.

RISK MANAGEMENT

Collaboration has been a primary risk mitigation strategy. It has helped us overcome the challenges of funding and skill deficits. Partnerships with leading technology companies and sanitation providers have allowed us to pioneer several geospatial projects to bridge the sanitation data gap, as in the following examples:

- We are resident innovators at Geovation, the U.K. Ordnance Survey's hub for location data, enabling us to learn from and utilize the skills of pioneers in geospatial science.

- We have received mentorship from IBM Emerging Technology.

- Morrison Foester has helped us with legal work, including our data-sharing agreements.

- KPMG's data science team participated in our data dive for urban sanitation.

Our sanitation data hubs face two primary risks. First, organizations could withdraw from the hub. This risk is low. Partner organizations have been involved in the design of the project from the start. Our team speaks with each member every two weeks to ensure that any concerns are quickly identified and addressed. Second, the municipal government may not have the personnel and financial capacity to act as the primary owner of the hub activities beyond the lifetime of this project. This risk will be assessed by our team members, who will create a plan with each member of the hub to identify who will be responsible beyond the lifetime of the project and to draft a financial plan to support them.

IMPACT

The Antananarivo sanitation data hub will help improve the lives of 350,000 people. Our goal is for hub members to use the geospatial SFD for at least 50 percent of their investment and operational expansion decisions. We also expect each hub member to have achieved at least 80 percent adherence to the data standard. This means that they would use the standard when collecting data for 8 of the 10 indicators defined by the data standard for the location, volume, and transportation of waste.

Once the hub is successful in the 5th arrondissement, we will expand to the rest of Antananarivo before replicating in the other target cities. We will also track the effectiveness of hub members' data-driven investments to measure the decrease in disease outbreak. This will set us on track to achieve our 2025 goal to transform how sanitation is provided for at least 5 million people across four emerging cities.

ANNEX 2A. TEAM GATHER

Gather is a small team with expansive ambition. John Peter Archer and Lindsey Noakes met in November 2015, while working in international development. Three weeks later, with a shared belief that toilets change everything, they launched Gather. At the start of 2019, the team expanded. Luiz Rodrigues joined as data analyst after applying data science to improve the legal system in Brazil, and Fiona Watters, with a background in geospatial data, joined as research assistant.

Team Gather

Photo: Gather. The data scientists who joined us as we hosted the world's first data dive for urban sanitation for Lusaka, Zambia.

We actively champion diversity. We have a near 50:50 gender ratio across our staff, advisory panel, and board of trustees. Our data dive in 2018 also brought together an industry-defying level of participation of nearly 50 percent women, with a background in geospatial data, and one-third from minority backgrounds (figure 2A).

Gather is governed by a multidisciplinary board of trustees and receives strategic advice from a panel of expert advisers who work for organizations including Google, UNICEF, and the Kounkuey Design Initiative. Gather is a resident innovator at Geovation, the U.K. Ordnance Survey's location data hub.

Gather is supported by a core group of private philanthropists from the United Kingdom. In 2018, we received grants from the Vitol Foundation and former U.S. Vice President Al Gore's Generation Foundation. In 2019, we are receiving support from the World Bank's Data Innovation Fund and the United Kingdom's Department for International Development's Small Charities Challenge Fund.

In 2018, Gather was recognized by Forbes 30 Social Entrepreneurs Under 30 in Europe and MIT Technology Review's 35 Innovators Under 35 in Europe. Gather also reached the finals of the Comic Relief Tech4Good for Africa Award.

REFERENCES

Artelia Madagascar. 2014. *Elaboration du Schéma Directeur d'Assainissment Urbain du Grand Tana*. Grand Tana: Arelia International.

Belton, Padraig. 2018. "Why Do Billions of People Still Lack Basic Sanitation? BBC News, April 23. https://www.bbc.co.uk/news/business-46289654.

UN-Water. 2018. *Sustainable Development Goal 6: Synthesis Report on Water and Sanitation 2018*. New York: United Nations.

WHO (World Health Organization), and UNICEF JMP (United Nations Children's Fund Joint Monitoring Programme). 2015. "Madagascar Household Data," WASH database, https://washdata.org/data/household#!/mdg.

World Bank Group. 2017. *Reducing Inequalities in Water Supply, Sanitation, and Hygiene in the Era of the Sustainable Development Goals: Synthesis Report of the WASH Poverty Diagnostic Initiative*. Washington, DC: World Bank Group.

3 WellPower: A Sustainable and Scalable Approach to Addressing the Water Crisis in Kenya Using an Innovative Smartphone App–Based Clean Water Delivery Network

BETHWEL KIPLIMO, *Cofounder, operations and integration. Mechanical engineering, Class of 2021*

TODD BALDWIN, *Cofounder, hardware and operations. Chemical and biological engineering, Class of 2020*

NOAH SCHOCHET, *Cofounder, business development and marketing. Mechanical engineering, Class of 2021*

AYUSHI SINHA, *Cofounder, software development and product management. Computer science, Class of 2020*

BAYO OKUSANYA, *Business strategy and finance. Philosophy, Class of 2020*

RONNIE KIHONGE, *Operations and integration. International relations, Class of 2022*

ABSTRACT In Kenya, 90 percent of adults have smartphones, yet 60 percent of the population still lacks access to piped water. WellPower is a start-up focused on clean water delivery using smartphones in Kenya. Governments in the developing world are unable to provide the necessary infrastructure to supply piped water to over 60 percent of the population, forcing them to pursue private sector solutions. Existing private solutions are too expensive and too inconvenient, and the water they provide is often of unsafe quality.

For years, other companies have focused on producing clean water. WellPower understands that the real problem is water distribution, which accounts for 90 percent of the cost of clean water. We reinvent water distribution with an app

Team WellPower, United States. All team members are Princeton University students.

that connects customers to deliverymen at the push of a button for fast, affordable, and convenient clean water delivery. First, customers place an order for clean water through a smartphone app, then a motorcycle deliveryman receives the order and is directed to the nearest safe water kiosk partner in our network to retrieve the water. Then he delivers it directly to the customer's doorstep.

WellPower is a pipeless water distribution network that is decentralized, digital, rapidly scalable, and economically sustainable. By digitizing this process we remove inefficiencies in water delivery, resulting in a cost-efficient distribution model that enables end users to get clean water conveniently and at an affordable price.

Terms used

boda boda = Motorcycle taxi delivery person

jerry can = The standard unit for water consumption in East Africa. Also known as a *mtungi,* it is a 20-liter (5.28-gallon) container for water, usually made of plastic, or a found container (formerly for oil or chemicals).

PROBLEM

Of the 44 million people in Kenya, 19 million still do not have access to clean water.[1] Like many people in Sub-Saharan Africa, Kenyans struggle daily to get water for their drinking, cooking, cleaning, and sanitation needs (see figure 3.1). The United Nations Children's Fund (UNICEF) reports that 200 million hours are spent by women and girls every day collecting water (UNICEF 2016). These hours detract from their ability to pursue an education or a career.

Beyond being inconvenient and difficult to access, water sources are often unclean and unsafe. Waterborne illness is the cause of 80 percent of all death and disease in the developing world (UN 2003) as well as 60 percent of all hospital visits and 10,000 infant deaths annually in Kenya (Namale 2014). Poor health reduces worker productivity and increases health care expenses for many households. With the average monthly wages in Kenya only K Sh 6,498 (US$76) (Macharia 2013), removing the burden of expensive, unnecessary hospital visits would do much to increase the standard of living. The United Nations estimates that for every US$1 invested in improving access to clean water, there will be a return of up to US$34 in economic benefits (Hutton and Haller 2004)—and that was before a solution as efficient and economically stimulating as WellPower was available.

FIGURE 3.1

Proportion of regional population with access to improved water across Africa, 2015

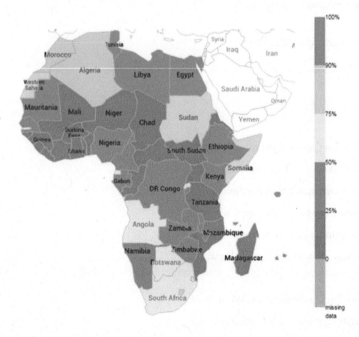

Source: WHO and UNICEF Joint Monitoring Programme for Water Supply and Sanitation, as cited in Robinson, Lunn, and Moses 2016.

MARKET OPPORTUNITY

As a leader in technological advancement in East Africa, Kenya is an appreciable market for WellPower's solution. Kenya has a network of 600,000 boda boda drivers, who provide inexpensive transportation for people and sometimes goods. Kenya also has deep mobile phone penetration, with 90 percent of the adult population owning smartphones and 93 percent equipped with mobile payments through M-Pesa, a mobile payment platform built into the SIM card. These conditions, combined with rapidly falling solar prices, which have experienced a 73 percent decrease since 2010, position WellPower to make a significant impact on clean water access in Kenya (figure 3.2).

The most common method of water retrieval in rural Kenya, where 74 percent of the population live, is the traditional method of getting water directly from rivers by collecting it in jerry cans (20-liter water containers).[2] This water is largely unsafe, because of contaminants from animal waste, human waste, and runoff.

For low-income urban dwellers, the most common method of water retrieval is through water stations or kiosks that are located close to private water wells. The water is distributed to households by carts driven by family or friends. Delivery can be unreliable, and the water is often unclean and expensive. Middle- to high-income Kenyans in urban settings rely on piped water, but it is also usually unclean, so they supplement it by buying bottled water for drinking. At US\$3–US\$5 per 20-liter container, this solution is an option that only 15 percent of Kenyans can afford (Wambui 2018; Cook, Kimuyu, and Whittington 2016).

Kenya's middle class is growing much faster than the infrastructure to support it. Given the above-mentioned conditions, this growth will create a large consumer base with a desire for convenient, clean water and money to pay for it. As WellPower saves people time and money, while also creating jobs in the middle of a technological revolution, the number of people who will pay to incorporate safe

FIGURE 3.2

Market size for the WellPower solution

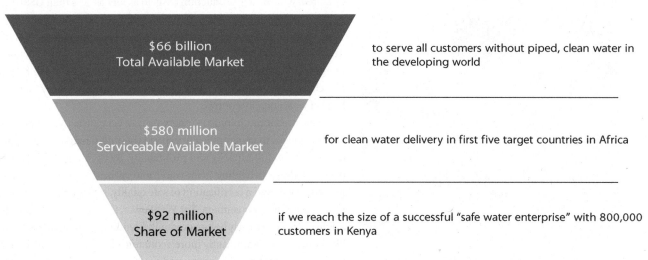

Total Available Market — \$66 billion — to serve all customers without piped, clean water in the developing world

Serviceable Available Market — \$580 million — for clean water delivery in first five target countries in Africa

Share of Market — \$92 million — if we reach the size of a successful "safe water enterprise" with 800,000 customers in Kenya

Note: In Kenya, safe water enterprises are businesses that sell filtered or purified water to customers.

drinking water into their lives will constantly increase, resulting in an expanding market.

SOLUTION

Our solution is a digital distribution network where customers place orders for clean water through a smartphone app. A motorcycle deliveryman (600,000 of whom already exist in Kenya) receives the order and is directed to the nearest safe water kiosk partner in our network to pick up the requested number of 20-liter jerry cans full of clean water. These cans are then delivered to the customer's doorstep. All payment is processed through the app via M-Pesa (a national mobile payment platform).

By eliminating most of the inefficiencies in the current water distribution systems, we are able to deliver safe water to our customers up to 50 times cheaper than bottled water, all at the touch of a button. WellPower provides a cheaper, safer, and more convenient way to get water, which is exactly what the customer wants.

Water filtration

As a team of four Princeton University engineers, we designed and deployed an ultra-low-cost solar-powered filtration system to be run by local Kenyan entrepreneurs. Self-cleaning and durable, our water filter is built to be physically and economically sustainable. Sales picked up as expected, but people were still limited by long walking distances. We learned that, in order to create the impact we desired and to prepare for fast expansion, our first step should be creating efficient delivery.

The WellPower team returned to Kenya during the summer of 2019 to deploy a digitized distribution infrastructure that sources water from existing kiosks (figure 3.3). It will allow us to scale rapidly at an extremely low cost. Once we have capital and customers, we will build our own kiosks when and where we know they will be economically sustainable. Having our own filtration systems, which will be locally operated, will cut our production costs to as low as less than US$0.02 per unit, increasing our margins and allowing us to expand our customer base to the lowest income tiers while providing the profits to further develop our technology and generate a strong return on investment. It will also give us control over water production and the filling and cleaning of bottles, and it will enable us to implement the highest level of water quality control.

In the meantime, joining our network is a very attractive option for existing kiosks to geographically expand their own markets, bringing them closer to full capacity and profitability. By becoming WellPower partners, these struggling "safe water enterprises" gain efficient delivery services and a certification of safe quality, making their product more desirable to consumers. For WellPower, the strategy to establish a delivery network early before gradually blending in our own filtration kiosks makes us significantly more economically viable, less risky, less reliant on capital requirements, and more likely to succeed at scale. (See figures 3.4, 3.5, and 3.6.)

FIGURE 3.3

A safe water kiosk, similar to the ones we will partner with in our network

Photo: Sanitation Alliance, used under Creative Commons license, https://creativecommons.org/licenses/by/2.0/deed.en.

Software

The software component of WellPower is a two-sided marketplace. It facilitates a process in which users place an order for water, and which is then assigned to a boda boda for delivery. In its ideal implementation, this software does the following:

- Customer
  - Takes customer orders
  - Processes payment using a mobile payment platform called M-Pesa
  - Facilitates easy use of referral programs through WhatsApp and social media

- Backend
  - Uses an algorithm to sort and assign orders to drivers
  - Uses an algorithm to plot the most efficient delivery route for each driver
  - Provides dashboard with data analytic insights
  - Provides each kiosk partner with a tablet-based dashboard to track and fill orders, receive demand predictions for the next day, and receive payment for supplying the water.

- Driver
  - Provides drivers with navigation to the delivery location
  - Pays drivers accordingly for their deliveries
  - Facilitates easy use of referral programs through WhatsApp and social media

One possible approach to introducing the app would be to build out the ideal implementation mentioned above in the form of a full stack Android smartphone app. This app would provide maximum functionality to users, the company, and drivers. However, this approach presents several drawbacks. First, users are reluctant to download new apps, because downloading and using a new app consumes data, which Kenyans purchase on a pay-as-you-go model (buying a few days' worth of data at a time rather than locking into a monthly subscription like most plans in the United States). Second, not all Kenyans have Android smartphones. Ten percent of Kenyan adults do not have smartphones, and not all smartphones run on Android (or even iOS) operating systems. Third, this application would be expensive and time consuming to completely build out, and it would be very risky to build out an entire app without customer testing and feedback, because

FIGURE 3.4

WellPower team in front of a solar-powered water filtration system we designed, built, and implemented

Photo: WellPower.

FIGURE 3.5

Water before and after going through our filtration system

After our filtration system

Before being filtered

Photo: WellPower.

FIGURE 3.6

A potential delivery network map, including WellPower kiosks, partner kiosks, and drivers

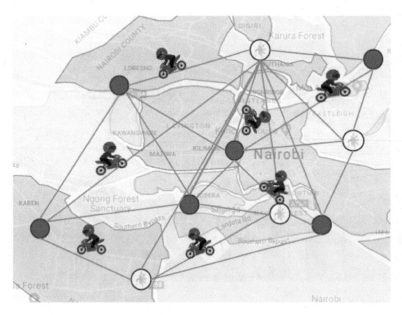

Note: The purification points act as nodes. The driver optimizes efficiency by refilling water from the closest node in the network. WellPower kiosks are indicated by WellPower's water and sun logo; blue dots denote kiosks operated by partners. Motorcycle icon by Emoji One used under Creative Commons license, https://creativecommons.org/licenses/by-sa/4.0/deed.en.

it is likely that the app would have to be designed to accommodate user feedback.

With these considerations in mind, WellPower will begin by building a minimum viable product (MVP). This MVP will allow us to quickly and cheaply design and test the core functions of the app in a simplified version before building out the entire application. It will use SMS and WhatsApp message-based ordering systems. The backend would be similar to or the same as the ideal implementation.

Building an MVP has several benefits. First, it allows us to receive and incorporate user feedback throughout the entire design process. Second, the MVP would be valuable as a stand-alone app even after the full Android app is built. The MVP relies on SMS (texting), so it consumes very little data; users who do not want to download the app out of data usage concerns could continue to use the MVP (although we would build it out to be more robust and polished). Third, customers who do not have a smartphone or an Android-based operating system would still be able to place orders for water and use our service (see figure 3.7). Last, using a WhatsApp bot to take orders has an added benefit of being easy to share and promote.

FIGURE 3.7

Screenshots of consumer-facing android smartphone application

Create an account. | Link your M-Pesa mobile payment account. | Set your delivery location. | Choose number of jerry cans. | View price estimate and confirm order.

Photos: WellPower.

We are already running a chat bot that facilitates ordering and payment on WhatsApp and SMS through twilio.org, a digital communications platform with a mission to serve businesses like WellPower that will seek to produce social good. We are also testing our Android-based app and receiving feedback from customers. All of this software uses cloud-based server space, making it highly scalable and affordable.

BUSINESS MODEL

Our business model centers on creating the most efficient production and distribution system for clean water in an East African context. WellPower will build and own the hardware (after the first one to two years), develop the software, and contract out delivery to independent contractors. Our main revenue stream initially will be sales of purified, delivered water to local businesses and households. Additional revenue streams in the future will take advantage of other economically productive uses for our energy infrastructure and distribution network.

Within our target market of Kenya and East Africa, we had several options for target customers. The first decision we faced was whether to sell to businesses or individuals. Our system can serve both with the same system architecture, and both need clean water delivered at an affordable rate. The major difference is in the customer acquisition strategy and costs and how they affect our solution's ability to scale.

Our research and surveys indicate that the best option for WellPower is to enter the market selling to businesses and then, after securing a solid foothold and revenue stream, begin to sell to individuals as well. This plan enables us to overcome the greatest failure point for water improvement projects, which is failing to create a sustainable business model. The first target customer business would be a tech-forward company in an urban environment that needs safe drinking water for its employees. The second target customer would be a small- to medium-size restaurant or café.

The first reason to target businesses initially is that, as a small team on a lean budget, we would find it much easier and cheaper to acquire local businesses as customers than individuals. One reason is that our representatives can go directly to the business and speak with the key decision maker or purchaser (the office manager or the owner of a restaurant). These customers have clearly defined needs that our product addresses and metrics for assessing our product's effect on their business. Delivered water saves them time, and ordering through a simple app eliminates hassle. Beyond that, both types of customers have a deep need for clean water. Companies need to provide their employees with clean drinking water. Café and restaurant owners need to provide clean drinking water to their customers because if a customer gets sick from dirty water even once, he or she will assume it was from bad food and never return to the restaurant again. In addition, when we sell to businesses we will have a consistent, predictable demand for large amounts of water, which translates into recurring revenue. Acquiring one company as a customer means daily water demand for 50–500 individuals. Acquiring one café or restaurant translates to roughly 150,000–300,000 liters annually. This amount translates to about 20–40 jerry cans per day, generating US$5–US$10 daily revenue (US$1,825–US$3,650 annually).

WellPower will sell to businesses to establish a foothold in the clean water market, generating enough revenue to be self-sustaining, covering the capital costs of building out a network of filtration systems, developing software, and establishing a driver network. With these key pieces in place, WellPower will have achieved the scale, stability, cash flow, and economies of scale to then sell to households. Selling to households will allow us to more directly accomplish our social mission.

Households are categorized by their purchasing and spending habits and abilities regarding water.

- Tier 1 is made up of lower-income families in rural Kenya who do not currently pay for water, because they are either unwilling or unable to do so, and they consume unfiltered water. This water is usually contaminated.

- Tier 2 consists of average-income families who understand, importance of convenient, purified water. Their preferred water sources include water stations or kiosks located close to private water wells. This water is distributed to homes on donkey carts driven by family or friends. Delivery can be unreliable and, despite claims of filtration, the water is often unclean, so tier 2 households treat their water using at-home filters, boiling, and chlorine tablets.

- Tier 3 is made up of the highest-income households, which rely on piped water. The piped water is usually unclean, so households usually supplement it by buying bottled water, which only 15 percent of Kenyans can afford (Wambui 2018; Cook, Kimuyu, and Whittington 2016).

Our business plan is to target tier 2 and tier 3 customers, because they already have the desire to consume purified water and are willing to pay for it if there is an affordable option such as WellPower. We will reach tier 1 households through partnerships with the public sector, nonprofits, or nongovernmental organizations (NGOs). It is also theoretically possible to eventually provide subsidized water to tier 1 to further our social impact mission once we achieve scale, according to our rigorous financial models. (See figure 3.8 for the economics of our plan.)

FIGURE 3.8
WellPower's improving unit economics over time

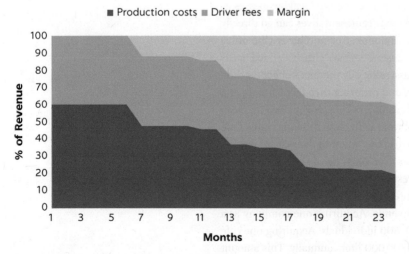

Note: The changes to WellPower's overall margins are a result of decreasing per unit production costs. In the early months, WellPower will buy water at market price from safe water kiosks. The production cost declines over time as we negotiate bulk order deals with kiosk owners and gradually blend in production from our own solar-powered hardware.

MISSION AND THEORY OF CHANGE

WellPower seeks to provide clean, affordable water to the people of Sub-Saharan Africa by using an efficient water filtration system coupled with an innovative distribution model. We believe that providing clean water and energy is the first step in the push for socioeconomic development in Africa. The technology exists to build a better future. All that is missing is a creative, strategic business model. By removing high levels of inefficiency and using an innovative business model, we will be able to provide clean water at the lowest possible price and serve the largest number of people.

With clean water for all, we will see a significant increase in economic growth. We will reduce household expenditures on clean water (which consume up to 50 percent of income) and medicine/health care. We will create jobs and stimulate local economies, hiring female operators for the systems and employing boda boda drivers, who will earn up to three times their daily income working many fewer hours. The increase in disposable income and savings will in turn lead to a higher marginal propensity to consume, which would magnify economic benefits and lead to rapid growth. Constant access to safe drinking water and sanitation opportunities will increase health and life expectancy. Without having to spend time transporting water, more women will get the chance to pursue education and work. WellPower will also create job opportunities for system operators and increase work for boda boda drivers, stimulating local economies and encouraging tech-based skills and entrepreneurship.

COMPETITIVE LANDSCAPE AND COMPETITIVE ADVANTAGE

For decades, entrepreneurs, impact investors, governments, and philanthropic organizations worldwide have been experimenting with solutions that complement traditional utility approaches to expand access to safe drinking water. Typical solutions addressing the clean water problem are stagnant in achieving the sustainability goals necessary to meet Kenya's commitment to achieve universal and equitable access to safe and affordable drinking water for all by 2030.

WellPower stands apart from the competition by providing the only solution that addresses the four main hurdles to universal and equitable access: clean water filtration, sustainability, delivery, and a tech-enabled solution (see figure 3.9).

FIGURE 3.9
WellPower's advantage over competitors

Typical Solutions

Competitors and Alternatives	Clean Water	Sustainable	Delivery	Tech-Enabled
Water utilities, bottled water	✔	✔		
Jibu, Engineers Without Borders	✔	✔		
LifeStraw, chlorine tablets	✔			
Water kiosk	✔	✔		
Uber, Taxify, current boda boda		✔	✔	✔
WellPower	★	★	★	★

FIGURE 3.10

WellPower's position in the market as most affordable and most convenient option

Customer behavior determined by price, convenience, and perceived quality

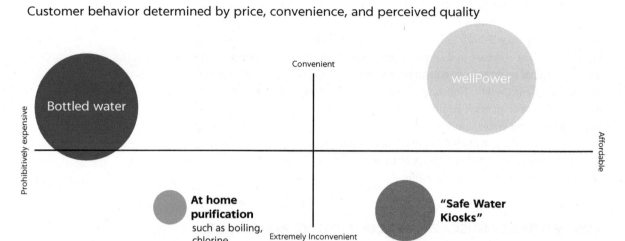

** Bubble Size Indicates Relative Water Quality/Safety.

Current solutions fail for a variety of reasons. First, many water solutions rely on poor or outdated technology, which make them too slow, too expensive, and too ineffective and require the use of harmful chemicals. Second, most previous efforts to provide clean water at scale failed to create a sustainable business model, often perpetually relying on donations or simply running out of capital. Almost half of water improvement projects are inoperable after only two years, usually because of lack of funding for operations and repairs. Third, most solutions to clean water fail to establish a delivery system. The delivery (or retrieval) of clean water is 90 percent of the financial or opportunity cost of water. Any solution that fails to include delivery can solve only 10 percent of the real problem. According to our customer surveys, affordability is the single biggest factor affecting the customer's decision to adopt a clean water solution. To scale a solution to this massive water problem, the developers of a clean water program must make it safe, convenient, and affordable (see figure 3.10).

TRACTION

WellPower was founded in November 2017. Our team began with a deep dive into the problem, studying which prior solutions had worked and which had failed. We met with more than 48 industry experts and professors. During that time we developed our theory of change and technology. We competed in and won several competitions (including second place in the Impact Summit, second place in PSICOMP, and finalist for the Hult Prize), which enabled us to strengthen our team, further develop our ideas, and make valuable connections while getting important feedback. We raised US$25,000 from a mix of competition prize money, friends and family (through GoFundMe), and school grants. This money allowed us to build three iterations of our working prototype. We took the third prototype to Kenya in December 2018 to deploy a pilot system. We also created a video summarizing some of the highlights, which can be viewed at https://www.youtube.com/watch?v=0SOXfor_jkA.

We deployed our pilot project in Emening, Kenya, the hometown of our cofounder Bethwel Kiplimo. There we met with local community leaders (including the chief), conducted in-depth site visits and customer surveys, and performed thorough research on our market. We then built our water filtration system. We began the process of hiring operators to run the system, created a system for processing payment, developed a pricing schedule, created training videos and maintenance manuals, and provided plenty of spare parts. We inaugurated our system with a community launch party, to which we invited the entire community to see the new system and get free water for one week. The village chief, a local senator, a community health official, and several other prominent figures spoke on our behalf to launch the new system. After deploying the system, we met in Nairobi with the top executives or founders of more than 25 companies and organizations to forge partnerships, build relationships, and learn as much as possible about the business ecosystem in Kenya (see figure 3.11).

Recently, the team has focused on our return to Kenya during summer 2019, when we will deploy a full rollout of our distribution model into a major Kenyan market. WellPower received an investment from Nate Faust, the cofounder of Jet.com (fastest company in history to reach US$1 billion valuation). This investment will allow us to finish product development and run a private beta in August 2019 for 50–200 customers, 5–15 drivers, and 1–3 kiosk partners. To meet the demands

FIGURE 3.11

Timeline of project from November 2017 to summer 2019

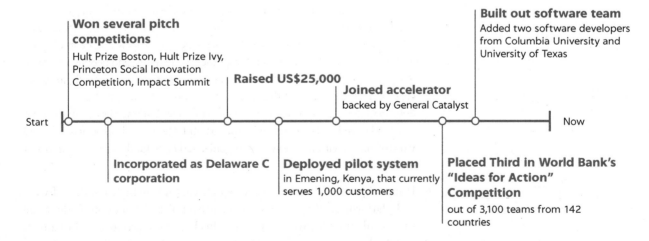

of this next step, WellPower has grown to include two software engineers as well as a ground team in Kenya. We are constantly on the lookout for talented new members.

PLAN TO SCALE

WellPower believes that in order to achieve our mission, it is essential that we serve a large number of people in a relatively compressed period. To do this, we will focus on starting with a software-heavy, asset-light business model to prove the concept and scale quickly early on. While it may be difficult to remain an exclusively software-based company in an African context, WellPower will always place emphasis on staying as lean as possible. Here is an outline of our plan to achieve scale over the next five years, although we will remain flexible as we grow, learn, and encounter new information:

1. Develop a simple Minimum Viable Product (MVP), a barebones software app.

2. Raise an angel investment round.

3. Take the MVP around to potential customers. Receive feedback on the app and use it to iterate. Conduct interviews to narrow our target customers and identify earliest adopters. During this process, collect as many preorders or letters of intent (LOI) as possible.

4. In the context of a small-scale private beta test (50–200 customers), develop and perform multiple low-cost experiments to test our hypotheses and validate any assumptions of our model. (What is the best pricing model: flat rate, subscription, variable pricing with distance? How much is our target customer willing and able to pay? Who are the ideal customers: corporations, local businesses, or individuals? Who will not want us entering the market, what could they do to stop us, what can we do to protect against that, and is there a cooperative way both parties could benefit?)

5. Our private beta will create a lot of hype, media, and word-of-mouth attention. Rather than rapidly letting everyone onto the platform and potentially becoming overwhelmed by demand, create a holding pen where interested customers can sign up for a waitlist or preorder. A strong way to do this would be to give our beta testers two to five invites each that they could use to add people directly to the platform without sitting on the waitlist. Every time we are ready for more customers, we can repeat the same tactic. This technique will grow us from 200 customers to 1,200 customers if each original customer invites five others. A second round will take us from 1,200 to 7,200. Media stories, social media, and word of mouth will create low-cost, organic marketing for the earliest stage of our growth.

6. Using this customer and market research, continue to build out the software and platform. At this stage, we have proven the distribution model to be successful and effective. We can use this highest degree of proof to attract partnerships. There are several thousand automated water dispensers (water ATMS) and water kiosks in Kenya, operating at 50 percent of their capacity. They already own and understand the hardware and maintenance of water

filtration, but they have too few customers. By partnering with them, we offer last-mile delivery for their water, giving them access to a much larger customer base without asking them to change any of their practices. This benefits both the kiosks/ATMs and WellPower. It allows us to operate as asset-light or even asset-free. This low-capital approach will be the key to scaling rapidly.

7. Simultaneously, we begin to raise our next round of investment using the success metrics and traction from steps 4 and 5 to attract investors. We will rely on two approaches. For the equity-based approach, we will look to African venture capital firms, impact investors, and high-net-worth individuals. For the equity-free approach, we will look to grants, foundations and organizations, philanthropy, and sustainable development funds.

8. We enact several aspects of our long-term plan for impact, addressing needs beyond clean water and incorporating additional revenue streams and services. Examples of how we can use our solar energy and distribution for economically beneficial ways are ice production and delivery or agricultural processing such as corn milling. This would allow us to further our mission of promoting sustainable development in Africa through technology.

9. The final step within a five-year horizon is to expand beyond Kenya. Initial countries to consider are Nigeria, Rwanda, South Africa, and Tanzania. Expanding beyond Kenya allows us to derisk our company from potential threats of political instability, conflict, or government interference. Any country can be unpredictable; a presence in multiple countries creates a diversified risk portfolio. Another benefit is access to new markets. It takes time to develop a new market, so we have to start early in order to stay ahead of competitors and entrants.

We expect WellPower to scale rapidly for several reasons. The first is the popularity of technological solutions, as well as the precedents set by companies like Uber and Taxify. Customers will be excited to order with an app, and they will be comfortable using our platform after experience with other app-based services. Given that our product is both profitable and socially beneficial, we are likely to attract individual investors who want returns on their investments so that they can continue investing in other start-ups. Once established in Kenya, we will be poised to expand into other countries that are prone to artificial water shortages and rapid increases in water price.

The second reason is that since we are software based, we are easily adaptable to many countries in the developing world. Drivers will be easy to recruit, because unemployment rates are high, profit margins with other companies are low, and the only requirement is owning a motorcycle.

The third reason is that technological advancements are likely to make operations cheaper and more efficient, as the prices of solar panels, high-tech filtration, electric vehicles, and high-quality cell coverage all drop. WellPower hopes to eventually deploy a complete fleet of electric motorcycles/bikes charged by free solar power, which would help drivers avoid gasoline costs and reduce emissions.

BENEFITS FLOW

WellPower offers immense benefits to the people of Sub-Saharan Africa across various sectors. We will have a positive effect on all our stakeholders. For beneficiaries, we will solve three main problems.

First, we will benefit the health sector by reducing instances of waterborne diseases. WellPower delivers water that is up to 99.99 percent purified, which means that there is virtually no chance of disease-causing pathogens in it. We disinfect our jerry cans after every cycle of distribution, eliminating the risk of postcontamination. Those steps will drastically reduce the incidence of waterborne diseases, which account for 80 percent of all deaths and disease in the region. The number of sick days will decline, increasing productivity. Kenya spends about US$627 million of its budget on the health sector. With waterborne diseases accounting for more than 60 percent of the hospital burden, reducing their occurrences will mean that Kenya will be able to invest this money in other sectors . The World Health Organization and UNICEF joint report shows that the water problem will save Kenya up to 50 percent of the health budget (Namale 2014).

Second, we will give back to women and children the 40 billion hours that they spend annually trying to get clean water, freeing them to get an education and build their careers. Women will have the freedom to spend time with their families or join the labor force. Women's participation in the labor force increases gross domestic product (U.S. Council of Economic Advisers 2019). Children will also be more skilled from the education they receive and therefore better equipped to build the country's economy.

Third, because of our efficient business model, we are able to offer clean water at very affordable prices. We sell purified, delivered water at just 2 percent of the cost of bottled water and 60 percent less than delivered, unfiltered water. People will therefore be able to retain 10 percent–50 percent of their income. They will also be able to save money that would otherwise be spent on paying medical bills from waterborne diseases.

WellPower is also greatly beneficial to the boda boda drivers who join the platform. They will receive up to three times more daily revenue while working 40 percent fewer hours. The reason is that much of their time was previously spent waiting for scarce customers to come by or making trips exclusively for one customer and driving back and forth four times per customer compared with one trip for six customers with WellPower. WellPower offers boda boda drivers consistent demand so they will always be driving back and forth whenever they are active. Their entrepreneurial culture will be enhanced, and they will have more disposable income to invest in their businesses.

Yet another benefit of our system is the income of the ground managers of our setups in different locations. WellPower will provide employment opportunities exclusively to women who will serve as ground managers. This job will elevate their status in society as income earners while also giving them an income to improve their living standards.

Our use of solar energy means that we have no negative effect on the environment. In the future, we hope to change our distribution to solar-powered electric motorcycles, eliminating the pollution and carbon emissions caused by motorcycles. WellPower will be carbon negative as soon as possible.

RISK AND RISK MITIGATION STRATEGY

Risk #1: Incorrect product market fit

WellPower is operating in a huge market that is rapidly expanding and underserved. The market is ripe for disruption, is lagging in tech/innovation, has no clearly dominant players, and does not serve a large portion of those in need. To ensure that our solution correctly addresses customer needs/wants, we have adopted a lean start-up model. With this type of model, we include our beneficiaries at every stage of the design process from the very beginning.

We also conduct inexpensive, efficient, and quick experiments to validate our assumptions and test our hypotheses. If each assumption and hypothesis that our solution is built upon is correct and supported by data, then it follows that the solution will be correct. We proved product market fit when we deployed our pilot system to 1,000 people in Emening, Kenya, in December 2018. We got direct feedback from the customer and proved there was willingness to pay for our solution.

We now have a platform to constantly test new features and ideas. This platform allows us to quickly and inexpensively experiment and validate future assumptions. Moving forward, we plan to build a team with a majority of members who live or grew up in our target markets. This plan ensures that we stay in touch with our beneficiaries as closely as possible.

Risk #2: Governmental intervention and political instability

On the basis of suggestions from several experts and executives with decades of experience in our market, we have created the following outline to mitigate governmental risk. We eliminated a large portion of this risk from the start by creating a solution that does not rely on any direct assistance or funding from the government. However, any company operating in an African country faces a risk that the government will step in and act against the company's interests. To address this possibility, we intend to focus on developing strong relationships with key players. We began this process when we went to Kenya in December 2018. We met with ministers of water and sanitation, local chiefs and administrators, tribal leaders, community organizers, and senators to open dialogues, create lines of communication, incorporate feedback and input, and establish aligned interests. We have also been advised to build out a strong legal team, and we have selected a shortlist of firms specializing in social entrepreneurs, foreign companies, governmental policy, and water rights. Our plan is to complement rather than compete with governmental interests, focusing on regions and populations that the national grid cannot serve.

Risk #3: Competition

We addressed existing competitors in the "Competitive Landscape" section of this chapter. There is also a long-term risk from potential entrants into the market. They are classified into two groups: established and homegrown.

Established competitors include companies like Uber, Lyft, and Taxify, which have the core technology to compete with last-mile delivery. These companies have extremely low penetration in Kenyan markets (and operate exclusively in Nairobi). Entering African markets requires modifications to strategy, product, and team that would hinder these firms' performance in their current markets. They focus on transportation of people and to a minor degree food; competing in the water market would require a large shift. If they decide to move into water (unlikely, but not impossible), we can protect ourselves by first using intellectual property protection. As the first mover in these markets, we qualify for and can establish such protection for many key components of our solution, including the hardware, software, and specific methodologies around the distribution system. Furthermore, we are pursuing exclusive agreements for distribution rights with the leading water kiosk and water ATM firms.

Homegrown competitors include any locals who try to replicate our model. We have a distinct advantage over these potential entrants given the highly technical nature of our system. Additionally, East Africa lacks the start-up ecosystem and funding system that WellPower has access to. It would be very difficult to raise the capital to start up exclusively within Kenya and nearly impossible to raise the capital required to scale without the access to U.S. capital that WellPower has.

Risk #4: Trust and reputation

When dealing with an essential good like water, customer trust is paramount. We can never compromise on quality and safety. We are able to earn the trust of our beneficiaries using multiple methods. The first step is to hire women at all levels of the organization, especially as operators of the systems. In Kenya, the key decision makers around water in each household are women. Hiring and empowering female operators builds trust with the female heads of households. The microfinance industry has generated a plethora of data to support the notion that women have higher rates of fiscal responsibility (Chakravarty, Iqbal, and Shahriar 2013).

It is also essential that our customers can trust our payment system. To do so, we integrated the nearly ubiquitous mobile payment platform M-Pesa into our app to handle all payments. Users can trust that 100 percent of their payment goes directly to us in an extremely secure manner and that we pay the drivers accordingly.

Users must also be able to trust that the water they order is from WellPower and uncontaminated. To ensure this condition, WellPower delivers water only in jerry cans that we own and clean between each use. Most jerry cans are found containers that previously contained oil, dirt, or chemicals. They are difficult for a household to properly clean and are poorly sanitized. By using our own clean, safe jerry cans bearing the WellPower logo and tracking number and sanitizing them thoroughly between uses, we can guarantee customers that if their water comes in a WellPower jerry can, it is safe to drink. We also rigorously test the water at regular intervals and post the results for the current batch of water on the app for all to see.

FINANCIALS AND COST BREAKDOWN

Assumptions

- **Drivers**
  - 1 boda boda normally works 12 hours a day and makes 20 trips. Drivers earn on average $10 a day and use that to pay their own expenses.
  - 1 boda boda can carry 6 cans per trip, 20 trips per day, leading to a capacity of 120 cans per driver per day.
- **Customers**
  - 1 customer is 1 household, comprising on average 4.08 people.
  - Each household demands five jerry cans of clean water per day.
- It costs US$12,000 per water purification system (24,000 liters per day, 1,200 jerry cans).
  - Each system is a node. We will create a mesh network of linked nodes (rather than fewer, larger centralized hub-and-spoke models) across a market to maximize coverage and distribution efficiency.
  - Each system serves 600 households (roughly equivalent to one rural village or one urban neighborhood).

Tables 3.1, 3.2, and 3.3 provide financial projections.

TABLE 3.1 **Optimistic but not unrealistic revenue scenario**

	1 month	6 months	12 months	18 months	24 months
Number of Drivers on Distribution Platform	5	49	134	368	1,009
Jerry Can Distribution Capacity, per Month	18,000	154,350	667,420	1,887,840	6,038,865
Number of Active Customers	100	904	2,972	9,178	27,695
Monthly Growth, %		23	21	20	20
Number of Jerry Cans Delivered to Households	15,000	135,600	445,800	1,378,700	4,154,250
Number of Jerry Cans Delivered per Month	15,000	135,600	445,800	1,376,700	4,154,250
Monthly Growth, %		23	21	20	20
Delivery Capacity, % of Total	83	88	65	73	69
Gross Sales to Household Customers	$3,750	$33,900	$111,450	$344,175	$1,038,563
Gross Sales per Month	$3,750	$33,900	$111,450	$344,175	$1,038,563
Average Price per Jerry Can Sold (All Customers)	$0.25	$0.25	$0.25	$0.25	$0.25
Less Delivery Fees from Household Deliveries	($1,500)	($13,560)	($44,580)	($137,670)	($415,425)
Delivery Fees Paid to Drivers	($1,500)	($13,560)	($44,530)	($137,670)	($416,425)
Total Gross Sales, %	(40)	(40)	(40)	(40)	(40)
Net Revenue Earned from Household Customers	$2,250	$20,340	$66,870	$206,505	$623,138
Net Revenue Earned by WellPower	$2,250	$20,340	$66,870	$206,505	$623,138
Average Net Revenue per Jerry Can Sold (All Customers)	$0.15	$0.15	$0.15	$0.15	$0.15
Average Net Revenue Per Customer (All Customers)	$22.50	$22.50	$22.50	$22.50	$22.50
Monthly Growth, %		23	21	20	20

TABLE 3.2 **Unit-level profit analysis for first 24 months**

	1 month	6 months	12 months	18 months	24 months
Number of Jerry Cans Delivered from 3rd-Party Sources	15,000	135,600	423,510	1,101,360	830,8050
Jerrys Delivered from WellPower Systems	0	0	22,290	275,340	3,323,400
Jerry Cans Delivered per Month	15,000	135,600	445,800	1,376,700	4,154,250
From 3rd-Party Sources, %	100	100	95	80	20
From WellPower, %	0	0	5	20	80
Cost to Acquire 3rd-Party Water (per Jerry Can)	($0.15)	($0.15)	($0.12)	($0.07)	($0.07)
Cost to Refill from WellPower System (per Jerry Can)	($0.02)	($0.02)	($0.02)	($0.02)	($0.02)
Blended Cost to Source Water for Delivery	($0.15)	($0.15)	($0.12)	($0.06)	($0.03)
Cost as % of Average Net Revenue per Jerry Can	100	100	77	40	20
Cost to Acquire 3rd-Party Water	($2,250)	($20,340)	($50,821)	($77,095)	($58,160)
Cost to Refil Jerry from WellPower System (per Jerry Can)	$0.00	$0.00	($445.80)	($5,506.80)	($66,468.00)
Cost to Build WellPower System	$0.00	$0.00	($1,493.33)	($17,955.00)	($213,966.67)
Cost to Source Water for Delivery	($2,250)	($20,340)	($52,760)	($100,557)	($318,594)
Net Revenue Earned by WellPower	$2,250	$20,340	$66,870	$206,505	$623,136
Less Total Cost to Source Water	($2,250)	($20,340)	($52,760)	($100,557)	($338,594)
Monthly Profit on Water Delivery, Excluding Operating Expenses	$0	$0	$14,110	$105,948	$284,543
Average Profit per Customer (All Customers)	$0.00	$0.00	$4.75	$11.54	$10.27
% Net Revenue Margin	0	0	21	51	46
Profit or Loss per Jerry Can Delivered after Fee	$0.00	$0.00	$0.03	$0.08	$0.07

Note: The table indicates initially purchasing water from the existing safe water kiosks to focus on rapid growth and then gradually transitioning to building WellPower's own hardware (already field tested) to cut costs and make the business profitable over a short period. All dollar amounts are U.S. dollars.

TABLE 3.3 **Costs of customer and driver acquisition**

	1 month	6 months	12 months	18 months	24 months
Number of Drivers Added per Month	5	8.4	22.6	62.2	170.6
Sign-Up Credit per New Driver	$5.00	$5.00	$5.00	$5.00	$5.00
Total Sign-Up Acquisition Costs Paid to New Drivers	($25)	($42)	($113)	($311)	($853)
Total New Household Monthly Customers Added	100	225	647	1,850	5,246
Sign-Up Bonus Paid to Driver (per New Customer)	$1.00	$1.00	$1.00	$0.50	$0.50
Total Customer Acquisition Costs Paid to Drivers	($100)	($225)	($647)	($925)	($2,523)
Total New Household Monthly Customers Added	100	225	647	1,850	5,246
Sign-Up Acquisition Costs Paid to Customer per Download	$2.50	$2.50	$2.50	$2.50	$2.09
Total Customer Acquisition Costs Paid to Customer	($250)	($564)	($1,618)	($4,625)	($10,492)
Total Driver Acquisition Costs	($125)	($267)	($760)	($1,236)	($3,476)
Total Customer Acquisition Costs	($250)	($5,564)	($1,618)	($4,625)	($10,492)
Total Acquisition Costs Paid by WellPower	($375)	($831)	($2,378)	($5,861)	($13,969)
Average Total Acquisition Cost per Customer Added	($3.75)	($4.95)	($4.64)	($3.81)	($3.05)
Average Net Profit per Customer over Next 2 Years	$103.28	$154.65	$195.96	$221.12	$246.58
Lifetime Value/Customor Acquisition Cost	27.54	31.26	42.19	58.06	80.94

Note: We give drivers a cash bonus for signing up. We use their customer network, paying them a referral fee for every customer they bring into our network. Our acquisition costs fall over time, whereas our net profit per customer increases, because of lower production costs and higher volume of sales. This model demonstrates how we will reach a critical mass of users and drivers. All dollar amounts are U.S. dollars.

WHAT'S NEXT

Upon successful completion of the pilot program, we will have validated our assumptions and proven the business model viable. Shortly after the pilot, we will raise an angel/seed round investment in order to continue to fund operations and fuel rapid growth. Beyond funding, we are also interested in developing potential partnerships. We are also looking for any contacts and connections in the region or in related fields. As our company grows, so must our team. We are looking for talented, driven individuals to join the WellPower family.

NOTES

1. For more information, see "Kenya's Water and Sanitation Crisis," Water.org, 2019, https://water.org/our-impact/kenya/.
2. See Trading Economics, "Kenya: Rural Population," 2016, https://tradingeconomics.com/kenya/rural-population-percent-of-total-population-wb-data.html.

REFERENCES

Chakravarty, Sugato, S. M. Zahid Iqbal, and Abu Zafar M. Shahriar. 2013. "Are Women 'Naturally' Better Credit Risks in Microcredit? Evidence from Field Experiments in Patriarchal and Matrilineal Societies in Bangladesh." Working Papers 1019, Purdue University, Department of Consumer Sciences, West Lafayette, IN.

Cook, Joseph, Peter Kimuyu, and Dale Whittington. 2016. "The Costs of Coping with Poor Water Supply in Rural Kenya." *Water Resources Research* 52 (2) https://agupubs.onlinelibrary.wiley.com/doi/full/10.1002/2015WR017468.

Hailu, Degol, Sara Rendtorff-Smith, and Raquel Tsukada. 2011. "Small-Scale Water Providers in Kenya: Pioneers or Predators?" United Nations Development Programme (UNDP), New York, August. https://www.undp.org/content/dam/undp/library/Poverty%20Reduction/Inclusive%20development/Kenya%20paper(web).pdf.

Hutton, Guy, and Laurence Haller. 2004. *Evaluation of the Costs and Benefits of Water and Sanitation Improvements at the Global Level*. Executive Summary. Geneva: World Health Organization. https://www.who.int/water_sanitation_health/en/execsummary.pdf.

Isaac, Korir. 2019. "Government's Budget for Health Sector Leaves Kenyans Spending Too Much Out of Their Pockets." *Soko Directory*, Hidalgo Investments Ltd. https://sokodirectory.com/2019/02/health-sector-budget-leaves-kenyans-spending-too-much/.

Macharia, James. 2013. "Kenyan MPs Defy President, Hike Pay to 130 Times Minimum Wage." Reuters, May 28. https://www.reuters.com/article/us-kenya-reform/kenyan-mps-defy-president-hike-pay-to-130-times-minimum-wage-idUSBRE94R0MW20130528.

Namale, Douglas. 2014. "Kenya: Water and Sanitation Ailments Kill 10,000 Infants Annually." *Mtaani Insight*, February 21. https://mtaaniinsight.wordpress.com/2014/02/21/kenya-water-and-sanitation-ailments-kill-10-000-infants-annually/.

Nyamai, Faith, and Collins Omulo. 2018. "Over 200 Kenyan Schools Shut as Water-Borne Diseases Rise." *Daily Nation*, May 21. https://www.nation.co.ke/news/Over-200-schools-shut-as-water-borne-diseases-rise/1056-4571930-r6ipq6/index.html.

Robinson, Tim, Jon Lunn, and Anna Moses. 2016. "Clean Water and Sanitation in Africa." Debate Pack CDP 2016-0086, U.K. House of Commons, April 18. https://researchbriefings.parliament.uk/ResearchBriefing/Summary/CDP-2016-0086.

Simmons, Ann M. 2016. "The World's Poorest Pay Largest Percentage of Income for Water, Study Says." *Los Angeles Times*, March 22. https://www.latimes.com/world/global-development/la-fg-global-world-water-story.html.

UN (United Nations). 2003. "'Water-Related Diseases Responsible for 80 Per Cent of All Illnesses,' Says Secretary-General in Environment Day Message." Press release, May 16. https://www .un.org/press/en/2003/sgsm8707.doc.htm.

UNICEF (United Nations Children's Fund). 2016. "Collecting Water Is Often a Colossal Waste of Time for Women and Girls." Press release, August 16. https://www.unicef.org/media /media_92690.html.

U.S. Council of Economic Advisers. 2019. "Relationship between Female Labor Force Participation Rates and GDP." The White House, Washington, DC, Feb. 27. https://www.whitehouse.gov /articles/relationship-female-labor-force-participation-rates-gdp/.

Wambui, Brenda. 2018. "The Kenyan Middle Class." *Brainstorm*, May 8. https://brainstorm.co.ke /2018/05/08/the-kenyan-middle-class/.

4 The Eco Panplas Solution

FELIPE CARDOSO, *Chief executive officer and founder*

THAINA HUGO, *Partner*

GUSTAVO EUGÊNIO, *Commercial director*

FABIAN CATTANEO, *Director of processes*

EVANDRO DIDONE, *Director of equipment*

SUMMARY

Ten million tons of plastic packaging end up in the oceans every year. This amount is the equivalent of 23,000 Boeing 747 aircraft in the seas and oceans—or more than 60 new planes landing on the seas every day, according to a report by the World Wildlife Fund (WWF 2019). According to World Bank figures, Brazil is the world's fourth-largest producer of plastic trash (Kaza and others 2018). At 11.3 million tons a year, it ranks behind only the United States, China, and India. Of that total, workers in Brazil collect more than 10.3 million tons, or 91 percent, but only 145,000 tons (1.28 percent) are actually being recycled—that is, reprocessed to enter the production chain as a secondary product. That 1.28 percent is one of the lowest figures anywhere and well below the global average for plastics recycling, which is 9 percent.

Landfills are the final destination of 7.7 million tons of plastic in Brazil. Another 2.4 million tons are discarded improperly, without any treatment, in open-air dumps. Pollution caused by plastic refuse affects the quality of the air, soil, and water sources. When burned or incinerated, plastic can release into the atmosphere toxic gases such as nitrogen dioxide and sulfur dioxide, both extremely harmful to human health. Plastics discarded in the open air can also pollute aquifers, bodies of water, and reservoirs, resulting in an increase in respiratory problems, heart disease, and damage to the nervous systems of people exposed to them (WWF 2019).

Eco Panplas believes people need to not only recycle more but also find ways to use less water in that process. For example, in Brazil alone, 40,000 tons of plastic motor oil packaging are discarded every year. Those containers still hold some residual oil—1.5 million liters (see figure 4.1). Just one liter of leftover oil can pollute 1 million liters of water.

Team Eco Panplas, Brazil.

For plastic refuse to be effectively recycled and transformed into a new product, it must first be decontaminated—that is, cleaned completely. Worldwide, cleaning has meant decontamination by washing with water. However, that solution does not work for a large portion of the contaminated plastics, the ones most likely to pollute the environment, because water will not efficiently remove the contaminant from the plastic. The use of thousands of liters of water generates effluents and various kinds of waste. That means that the process itself poses a significant environmental risk. Furthermore, the quality of the plastic deteriorates so that it is less usable and less economically valuable. Its value declines throughout the recycling chain, mainly in terms of the sums people are willing to pay for the waste gathered by trash pickers and cooperatives.

Imagine that you get your hands dirty while working with motor oil. Water will not be enough to get the oil off, so you use detergent to remove a little more. However, your hands will still be dirty, and the water you used will be contaminated with oil. The detergent you used will also be mixed with oil and the two together become hazardous waste. This is what happens when water is used for decontamination and recycling, which occurs on a large scale, thereby increasing the environmental risk.

Eco Panplas developed a technological solution that decontaminates and recycles plastic containers ecologically—without using water or producing waste. The process uses an ecological degreaser developed by Eco Panplas that can be separated from the contaminant, maintaining the characteristics of both. Therefore, we can recover the degreaser for reuse and the contaminant—the oil—for sale. The technology was developed in Brazil by Eco Panplas over a three-year period. It involves a high-capacity automated production line consisting of equipment that performs nine processes.

All the residual oil is recovered and recycled. It becomes a by-product and so eliminates the associated environmental hazard (see figure 4.2).

Even better, the process produces a recycled plastic of excellent quality that

FIGURE 4.1

Bales of used motor oil containers

Photo: Eco Panplas. Receiving area in Eco Panplas production plant.

FIGURE 4.2

Recovered motor oil

Photo: Eco Panplas.

can be made into new containers composed of 100 percent recycled material. The cost can be as much as 10 percent lower than other containers, thereby creating a true economic circle (see figures 4.3 and 4.4).

During the past two years, Eco Panplas conducted a pilot operation that processed 8 million containers, recovering and selling more than 400 tons of recycled plastic to make new motor oil containers and 17,000 liters of recovered oil that was sold for reuse. The operation resulted in significant socioenvironmental benefits (see figures 4.5 and 4.6).

The Eco Panplas solution is now well established in the Brazilian market. All its current and future output has been sold. The process has gained recognition because of the major Brazilian awards it has won. Twice it won the Eco Brasil prize; it also won the 2018 World Water Forum prize. Internationally, it won the 2018 Inter-American Development Bank-FEMSA award for innovation in water and sanitation given in Washington, DC and the 2019 Sustainable Development Goals (SDG) Award from the UN Global Compact.

We are now in a position to expand our solution using high-capacity production units installed in shipping containers that take up relatively little space (see figure 4.7). They can be located near high-volume sources of motor oil containers, facilitating all the logistics and scalability.

FIGURE 4.3

High-quality recycled plastic and recycled packaging at lower cost

Photo: Eco Panplas.

FIGURE 4.4

Eco Panplas technology (which separates all inputs) versus water washing

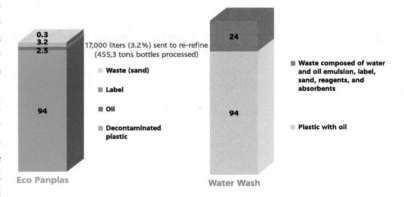

In Brazil alone, by installing 20 units distributed among seven production plants, we could immediately increase our lubricants-packaging capacity and increase our capacity tenfold to handle the volume being collected today and a hundredfold to handle the entire volume discarded on the market.

The next steps, therefore, are to grow and dominate the Brazilian market in lubricants packaging and to reach an international market. We will use partnerships, because this solution is a disruptive one that is unique in the world. We also plan to find new applications for other plastic waste and other markets.

FIGURE 4.5

High-capacity pilot plant that can produce 200 tons of uncontaminated plastic per month

Photo: Eco Panplas.

FIGURE 4.6

Socioenvironmental benefits from processing 400 tons of motor oil containers

 17 billion liters of water protected

 75% of energy saves

 430 tons of contaminated plastic out of landfills

 1,264 waste pickers required to collect this volume

 612 tons less greenhouse gas emissions

 120,000 liters of water avoided in the production

Source: Eco Panplas key performance indicators.

FIGURE 4.7

Compact units house the technology

Source: Eco Panplas rendering.

REFERENCES

Kaza, Silpa, Lisa C. Yao, Perinaz Bhada-Tata, and Frank Van Woerden. 2018. *What a Waste 2.0: A Global Snapshot of Solid Waste Management to 2050*. Washington, DC: World Bank.

WWF (World Wildlife Fund). 2019. "Brasil é o 4º país mundo que mais gera lixo plastic." WWF Brasil website, March 4. https://www.wwf.org.br/?70222/Brasil-e-o-4-pais-do-mundo-que-mais-gera-lixo-plastico.

5 Ekomuro H₂O+: Collecting Rainwater in Used PET Containers in Poor Urban Areas

RICARDO ALBA ALDANA, *Chief executive officer*

RICARDO ENRIQUE ALBA TORRES, *Chief operating officer*

NANCY TORRES BELLO, *Chief operating officer*

JESSICA BIBIANA ALBA TORRES, *Chief marketing officer—graphic designer*

ABSTRACT Water service is one of the basic needs of urban settlements and government housing projects on the outskirts of cities in Colombia. Homes in rural areas commonly have a system for storing rainwater; urban communities have space limitations, so rainwater storage is more difficult. Ekomuro H₂O+ proposes a vertical water tank system that reuses plastic bottles to store rainwater for such purposes as watering gardens and cleaning floors. The project aims to create a change of attitude on harvesting rainwater as a strategic natural resource for urban sustainability, risk reduction, and resilience building.

The Ekomuro H₂O+ project is a simple, innovative proposal based on the reuse of 3-liter containers made of polyethylene terephthalate (PET). The Ekomuro structure, which residents can make themselves, is designed in a modular way, takes up minimal space, and is made of nine towers of six 3-liter bottles each, connected to a PVC base.

The project began at public schools as a teaching proposal on the proper use of solid waste and the use of a natural resource. It has a cultural reference in communities, will reduce vulnerability, and will provide a mechanism of adaptation to climate change and water conservation.

Ecomuro H₂O, Bogotá, Colombia.

NARRATIVE

Situation before the initiative began

Urban communities do not have a culture of collecting rainwater. Public policy does not include educational programs that facilitate the comprehensive reuse of rainwater in the homes of urban residents. They are unaware that the use of rainwater is a strategic resource for adapting to climate change with environmental and economic benefits.

Establishment of priorities

From its beginning, the project sought to improve awareness of the use of natural resources and to put some types of solid waste to good use. Now that the project has started, it has generated a change of attitude in students and the community on good environmental practices. Priorities of the project include the following:

- Improve people's quality of life, which will be manifested in eco-efficient water saving and in making the most of the space they have.

- Be officially promoted and included in urban policy and educational programs.

- Be accepted in the community for the environmental, economic, and sustainable development benefits.

- Arouse interest in the community, so that people will implement the project in their houses by themselves.

- Give people individual and collective satisfaction for their contribution to good environmental practices.

- Generate a valid and eco-efficient option for purifying rainwater to be replicated at the local and regional levels (figure 5.1).

FORMULATION OF OBJECTIVES AND STRATEGIES

Fundamental objectives

Ekomuro H$_2$O+ seeks to encourage, promote, and strengthen good environmental and social practices by implementing rainwater collection systems in urban areas of poverty, improving their resilience and vulnerability.

Strategies

- Promote integration of the community around an innovative environmental initiative with inclusive and participatory characteristics that contribute to sustainable development.

- Free up space in homes by replacing conventional containers.

FIGURE 5.1

Purified rainwater can be used for drinking

Photo: Ekomuro H₂O+.

Note: In some Ekomuros, a sawyer filter, which works by reverse osmosis, is installed. The filter enables the rainwater to be purified. When installed together with an activated carbon and sand filter to make the filtering process more complete, the rainwater is safe for drinking. The systems can be installed in education institutions at the local and national level.

- Train community members in the proper development and implementation of Ekomuros and help them see in the project an income option for their families.

- Institutionalize an environmental initiative in schools, so that community members appreciate the schools' economic, environmental, and social successes and want to use them as an example to replicate in their homes.

- Facilitate knowledge transfer on the use of appropriate technology in an energetic and eco-efficient way that would lead the community to consider it as essential adaptation to climate change.

MOBILIZATION OF RESOURCES

Ekomuro H₂O+ established strategic alliances with public schools, a foundation called Fundación Santa Fe de Bogotá, and people who do recycling as their work, as well as with FUNLEO (Leo Espinosa Foundation) in eight different Bogotá locations. The aim was to diversify the initiative and encourage schools and homes to replicate the techniques. Financial resources were provided by the District Education Secretariat in its participatory budgeting programs for implementation of several projects developed in the academic year.

Ekomuro H₂O+ system at the Alfonso López Michelsen de Bogotá School, which irrigates the garden with rainwater

Photo: Ekomuro H₂O+.

Transformation Citizen Initiatives (INCITAR) through the District Education Secretariat will provide the financial resources to other public schools to replicate the project. Student members of environmental groups, teachers, and parents participated in the project (figure 5.2). Foundations that have an environmental and social responsibility focus have also used their own resources to help the population in other locations.

After winning the Eco-Challenge competition sponsored by PepsiCo and the Organization of American States (OAS), Ekomuro H₂O+ began implementing the first phase of a pilot project in Comuna 4 in Altos de Cazuca near Bogotá, where many vulnerable and displaced people in Colombia come to live. This first phase included the implementation of Ekomuros in 10 houses in two neighborhoods of the comuna to socialize the scope and benefits of Ekomuros to people (figure 5.3). PepsiCo Latin America and its sustainability manager endorsed this pilot project, approving budgets to benefit three headquarters of the Luis Carlos Galán School and 30 families whose homes lack water service.

PROCESS

Problems faced

Rain harvesting is an age-old activity, practiced by many cultures in areas of poverty and wealth. Urban communities in Colombia have discarded it because of ignorance and lack of education. The challenge is to change the lackadaisical attitude of the state agencies responsible for environmental policy and to make the population part of water saving, reduction of vulnerability, and adaptation to climate change through rainwater harvesting. The innovative environmental initiative promoted by Ekomuro H₂O+ consolidates the collection of rainwater into minimal space as an option in urban risks prevention.

Education

The dissemination of the project in schools and homes enabled educational communities to prove the effectiveness of using harvested rainwater in cleaning floors and toilets and in watering gardens. Awareness workshops at schools enabled students to differentiate between the concepts of recycling and reuse, with an emphasis on PET bottles. The reuse of PET does not generate any pollution and constitutes a valuable contribution to the reduction of this type of waste.

Action

The involvement of the Comuna 4 of Altos de Cazuca community in recovering PET bottles and using them in Ekomuros at their homes has generated a sense of opportunity among inhabitants. Less vulnerability and more resilience during periods of drought are evident. Observing the Ekomuros, neighbors wish to be included as project beneficiaries.

The Ekomuro works as a water storage tank, built with 36 plastic bottles interconnected through a PVC pipe base that enables each line of bottles to fill with rainwater from bottom to top. The bottles are perforated at the bottom and connected to each other by a hermetic seal made with PVC pipe and silicon. We perforate and attach two lids to each other to connect the tips (figure 5.4).

If schools and homes install Ekomuros to harvest rainwater and sustainable planning regulations are instituted for the care and preservation of water, more communities with a minimum standard of living will have water for sanitation and gardening.

RESULTS ACHIEVED

The pilot project of Ekomuro H₂O+ has achieved the following results:

- The living conditions of the inhabitants of Comuna 4 are better. They can gather rainwater and save it in an eco-efficient manner that also saves space. Ten families, including single mothers and children, benefited. Forty families who learned of the project's scope and purpose have registered and will benefit through a grant from PepsiCo Latin America.

- Project developers and students have participated in national and international fairs, allowing them to convey a message of environmental education and awareness of the use of natural resources and good use of waste to an estimated population of more than 100,000 people.

- With the implementation of the project in eight schools in Bogotá in 2014 and 2015, 20,000 people have more awareness of the culture of water harvesting and

FIGURE 5.3
Ekomuro at urban housing in Bogotá

Photo: Ekomuro H₂O+.

Note: The water at this location is used for domestic purposes—washing floors, watering plants, and toilet discharges.

FIGURE 5.4
Ekomuro water tank

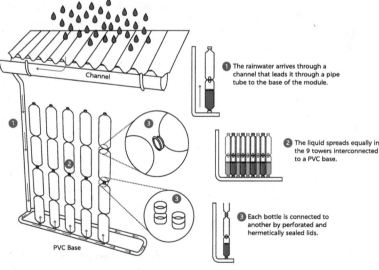

Channel

PVC Base

1. The rainwater arrives through a channel that leads it through a pipe tube to the base of the module.

2. The liquid spreads equally in the 9 towers interconnected to a PVC base.

3. Each bottle is connected to another by perforated and hermetically sealed lids.

reuse of waste. Schools are fundamental for the integral formation of students; in their facilities parents, teachers, and students interact. Our project makes strategic points to students and others about an initiative that meets social and environmental functions.

- Ekomuro H_2O+ has been recognized locally and internationally as an environmentally sustainable alternative. During the past four years of project development, the project has received the following awards: finalist in Google Science Fair 2012, nomination for Science in Action by *Scientific American*, winner of Eco-Challenge PepsiCo-OAS, finalist in Bayer Young Environmental Envoy, honorable mention from Youth Water Protectors—Pavco-Mexichem, and candidate for "Water for Life" UN-Water Best Practices Award 2014.

SUSTAINABILITY

Financial

In the early stages of the project in this vulnerable community, it was necessary to subsidize part of the supplies and logistics to implement the first phase. Later, the beneficiaries, grounded in the appropriate technology and training, contributed their labor and made rainwater canals, collected 3-liter PET bottles, and assembled the containers to end up building the system themselves.

Social and economic

Social inclusion occurs when people who work at recycling and improving the environment are valued. The project reuses PET bottles that people recover on the street and acquires them at fair value, dignifying their work. With this activity, families in some sectors of the comuna increased their income. Collected rainwater lowered the cost of water for home and garden work, created a bond between the community around the use of a natural resource, and gave people an individual and collective sense of environmental stewardship.

Cultural

Participation in national forums and fairs by students and members of school environmental committees allowed cultural interaction with other regions about scientific and technological problems related to water and recycling. Students in the project became more knowledgeable about and gained a more positive view of the use of natural resources. Other topics they learned about included recycling and reuse of waste, adapting to climate change and global warming, rain harvesting, alternative energies, resilience, and vulnerability.

Environmental

Appropriate technology and environmental education became complementary actions that generated a change of attitude in the comuna on the use of natural resources. Students realized that water is essential to health, human welfare, and the preservation of the environment. The actions, ideas, and initiatives of an individual or a collective are welcome anywhere in the world to contribute to this purpose. Students began to have an awareness of the importance of preserving water resources and using rainwater as a valid alternative to address these challenges.

LESSONS LEARNED

Ekomuro H₂O+ learned the following lessons from this pilot project:

- It is possible to generate an innovative, inclusive, and participatory initiative with social and economic benefits to the population. Environmental issues developed by the project should be considered as a way to recognize principles and clarify concepts for students. Students acquired skills and attitudes that are necessary to understand and appreciate the interrelationships between the individual and the environment. They participated in work based on concepts of sustainability and eco-efficiency, and their behavior toward the use of natural resources and recycling changed.

- It is possible to offer an environmentally innovative initiative to communities in areas of urban poverty and find out if they are willing to accept it to reduce their vulnerability, if they are considered as participant actors in behavioral urban changes, transforming social realities and improving their quality of life.

- It is possible to create strategic alliances with public entities, nongovernmental organizations (NGOs), and the private sector to generate economic resources to implement and spread an innovative project aimed at changing traditional water storage systems and complement environmental education in schools (figure 5.5). The project showed that it can be done in a dynamic, sustainable, and efficient way.

- It is possible, thanks to the Internet, to establish technological knowledge transfer links with other environmental initiatives. The issues addressed by Ekomuros can apply internationally and be replicated in other countries. Ekomuro H₂O+ can learn of experiences elsewhere as well.

FIGURE 5.5

Ekomuro construction project mobile toilets

Photo: Ekomuro H₂O+.

Note: This Ekomuro H₂O+ system was installed in a mobile toilet by the company Pavimentos de Colombia. The container is used at construction projects. The rainwater stored by the Ekomuro is used to discharge the toilets.

TRANSFERS OF KNOWLEDGE AND TECHNOLOGY

The implementation process of Ekomuros in public schools and urban housing has been described in blogs and news and media websites worldwide, including in the *Miami Herald*. The project has won awards and national and international prizes, which has helped generate sufficient credibility.

Various individuals and entities have replicatd the initiative.

- The 17th contest of the Environmental Protection Fund of the Ministry of Environment of Chile selected the replication and implementation of the Ekomuro H_2O+ project at the Escuela Altamira of Coyhaique in the Aysen region, promoted by the Universidad Austral de Chile.

- The Servicio de Tecnologías Alternativas (Alternative Technologies Service, SERTA) organization, located in northeastern Brazil, is a vocational agroecology school for youth and adults that implemented Ekomuros in its facilities.

- Tlachichilco Municipality, Veracruz, Mexico, won first place with its entry of collecting rainwater in an Ekomuro cistern of PET containers. The Municipal Presidency in Cadereyta, in coordination with Unidad de Servicios Para la Educación Básica en el Estado de Querétaro, or Unit of Services for Basic Education in the State of Querétaro (USEBEQ), entered the 14th Competition of Science and Technology in the Delegación El Palmar auditorium, where eight primary schools participated.

- The Universidad del Valle de Guatemala Campos del Sur, through the international organization Entrepreneurial Action Us (Enactus), which has a presence in 39 countries, wants to implement Ekomuros in a public school and some houses in three towns in the southern region of Guatemala.

- The selection of Ekomuro H_2O+ as a candidate for "Water for Life," the UN-Water Best Practices Award, in 2014 enabled transfer to other countries.

SOURCES OF FUNDS

Fundación Santa Fe de Bogotá: Implemented Ekomuros H_2O+ at rural public schools Torca and Verjon Alto within their programs of community health.

Leo Espinosa Foundation: Implemented the Ekomuro system for collecting rainwater in urban gardens on terraces in Comuna 4 of Altos de Cazuca.

Public Schools: Participatory budgeting complemented the environmental projects of the following schools: Colegio Alfonso López Michelsen, Antonio José de Sucre, Nicolás Esguerra, Marruecos y Molinos, Luis Vargas Tejada, Sorrento, Rural Las Violetas Usme.

Cooperativo Ismael Perdomo School: Implemented the largest Ekomuro built so far with purification system filters.

PepsiCo-OAS (Eco-Challenge Award 2013): As winners of the Talent and Innovation Competition (TIC) of the Americas 2013 promoted by the OAS and PepsiCo, we allocated 30 percent of the prize money to start the first phase of the pilot project to collect rainwater in used PET containers in Comuna 4 of Altos de Cazuca.

PepsiCo Latin America: At the request of the PepsiCo Latin America Sustainability Management Application to implement a pilot project in Colombia, the Ekomuro H_2O+ group with a social responsibility focus formulated the "Implementation Project Ekomuro H_2O+ Collecting Rainwater in Used PET Containers in Urban Poverty," whose budget included materials and supplies, strategic and logistical support, systems equipment, and installation in housing at Comuna 4 Cazuca Altos de Bogotá DC.

KEY DATES

July 2009: Implementation of project Ekomuro in three public schools in Bogotá.

August 2010: Implementation of project in first urban housing in Castilla neighborhood of Bogotá.

October 2010: Alfonso Lopez Michelsen School in Bogotá wins Water Care Culture Award promoted by the District Department of the Environment.

June 2012: Ekomuro is regional finalist representing Latin America at the Google Science Fair 2012, with a nomination to Science in Action award promoted by *Scientific American*.

June 2013: Ekomuros wins Talent and Innovation Competition (TIC) of the Americas/Eco-Challenge 2013, organized by the OAS and PepsiCo.

July 2013: The Universidad Nacional Autónoma de Honduras (UNAH) replicates the project at Escuela de Colonia Fuerzas Unidas, focusing on the Climate Change Mitigation Program of the UN Environment Programme (UNEP).

February 2014: First phase of pilot project implementation begins in urban poverty regions of Comuna 4 in Altos de Cazuca near Bogotá.

March 2014: Project is selected as a candidate for "Water for Life," UN-Water Best Practices Award 2014.

2015: Project wins award at World Water Challenge, Seventh World Water Forum, Republic of Korea, sponsored by Korea Environment Corporation and Daegu Metropolitan City.

2016: Project wins Premio Nacional de Ecologia Planeta Azul, Colombia, sponsored by Banco de Occidente.

2018: Project is regional finalist in the World Champions of the Earth, a program established by UNEP.

6 DamoGO: Implementation of Mobile App–Based Technology to Tackle Food Waste in the Republic of Korea and Southeast Asian Countries

HWANG SOO LYNN, *CEO and cofounder*

MUHAMMAD FARRAS, *Customer relations manager and cofounder*

KIM JUAN, *Sales and marketing manager*

ABSTRACT Most restaurants, bakeries, and grocery stores throw away up to 25 percent in net profit, adding up to 15 percent to their food costs. These businesses face an inevitable problem near closing time every single day: what to do with their perfectly good, unsold, surplus food. Most of the time, it ends up getting thrown away, wasting food and costing businesses money, as food businesses in the Republic of Korea pay for food waste by weight. One-fifth of all food produced in Korea ends up in the trash (Ministry of Environment 2018). Most unused food (84 percent) ends up in the trash (Verrill 2016). Some businesses try to donate the food to those in need. However, only 1.4 percent of restaurant food is donated (Verrill 2016). Logistical issues make it tough for owners to deliver the food to charity; it is much easier just to throw it away.

With these challenges in mind, we developed DamoGO, a mobile app that enables anyone to purchase and "rescue" unsold food (figure 6.1). Users can find highly discounted food based on location, at a minimum of 50 percent off the original price, and receive notifications in real time as soon as a store uploads an item. Users purchase this food directly from the DamoGO app. They also have the option to donate the food to those in need.

Team DamoGO Inc.

FIGURE 6.1
DamoGO technology plan to reduce food waste by partnering with food stores

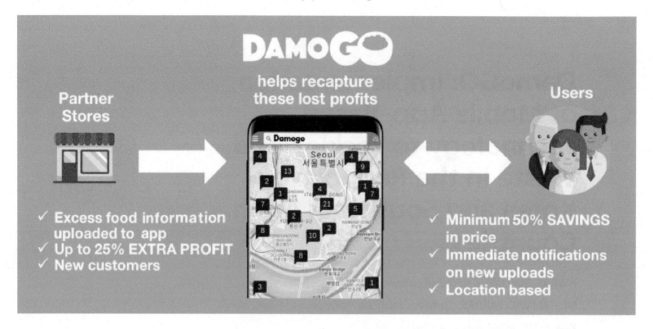

PROBLEM AND CONTEXT

Restaurants, bakeries, and food retailers cannot predict how much inventory of food to have on hand; most of these businesses overstock products because they do not want to run out. By the time businesses close for the day, the owners must figure out what to do with the unsold food. The following are real-world inefficiencies that food suppliers face:

- Pizza stores that make their own dough must make the dough 24 hours ahead of time, without knowing how much they will sell the next day. Unsold pizza dough gets thrown away. This revenue could be recovered by baking simple cheese pizzas if there were an outlet through which to sell them.

- Many sandwich stores bake their own bread every day without knowing how many sandwiches they will sell. This unsold bread could be sold at a discount as packs of loose bread or as low-cost, simple sandwiches.

- KFC and Dunkin' Donuts outlets in Korea also typically have unsold food items at the end of each day. KFC offers two-for-one after 9 p.m. to try to sell its unsold chicken. Dunkin' Donuts does so after 8 p.m. to sell its unsold donuts.

- Many restaurants accept delivery orders. When customers cancel the order after it is started, the restaurant has to absorb the loss. These canceled orders could be sold on our app instead of being thrown away.

- During bad weather, restaurants do not get many customers. Restaurants could begin uploading food at a huge discount throughout the day to reduce the amount of surplus food at closing time.

- Restaurants constantly test new menu items and are left with sellable food they cannot use. These items could be uploaded to our app at a discount.

- Restaurant sometimes prepare the wrong item. These orders usually end up in the trash. They could be uploaded to our app.

Korea has a population of approximately 51 million people, about half of whom live in the Seoul metropolitan area. The country has over 638,000 restaurants (Statista 2016), 220,000 food stores (KoreaStatistics 2017), 12,000 bakeries (Flanders Investment & Trade Seoul 2014), and 50,000 cafés. Seoul has one of the highest densities in the world of these businesses. These businesses throw away US$1.6 billion worth of sellable food every year. Given Koreans' increased awareness of social issues, the Korean government has a new initiative to reduce food waste (Ministry of Environment 2018).

Rising costs make it difficult for small- and medium-size enterprises (SMEs) to survive. A 2015 survey of SMEs showed that 75 percent faced difficulties running their business, 50 percent said that their monthly sales were down by at least 20 percent, and 90 percent said their work hours increased from the previous year (Seo 2018). Even with the government initiative to reduce food waste, the volume of waste in Korea has been rising by 3 percent a year. It currently stands at more than 14,000 tons per day. Every day, 2,000 tons of perfectly good food is thrown away.(Ministry of Environment 2018).

SOLUTION

DamoGO partners with restaurants and food retailers—marts, supermarkets, grocery stores, convenience stores, bakeries, cafés, and so on—signing them up to the store version of the DamoGO app. When partners have unsold sellable food, they open the app. In a few clicks, the item is uploaded for any DamoGO app user to see immediately. Once a user makes a purchase through the app, the business gets notification. When a customer comes to pick up the item, a clerk scans the QR code receipt on the customer's version of the app at checkout.

Users who have downloaded the DamoGO app can search for discounted food by location (figure 6.2). Users can also choose to receive real-time notifications

FIGURE 6.2
How the DamoGO app works

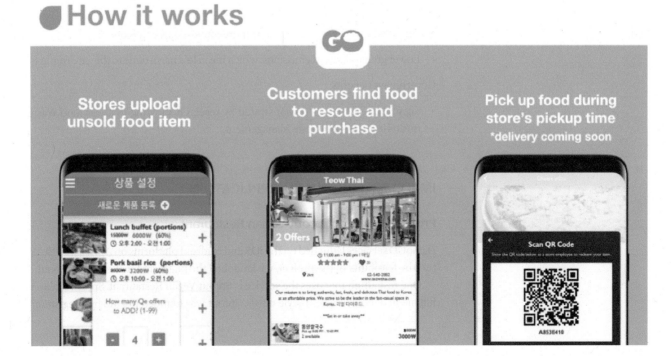

when items from their favorite stores are uploaded. This means users could be at school or work during the day and get instant notification when the restaurant next to their home uploads a pasta meal that is 50 percent off. The user could purchase it immediately and then pick it up during the store's pickup time. Every food item is at least 50 percent off the regular price. Users make purchases directly on the app. DamoGO keeps 25 percent of every transaction, and stores get paid the remaining 75 percent every month. There are no fees, and DamoGO users pay no service charge.

WHY PARTNER WITH DAMOGO?

DamoGO is a prime example of a win-win situation. There are benefits for everyone involved:

Restaurant and retailer benefits:

- Up to a 25 percent increase in net profit as a result of the sale of sellable food that would have been thrown away

- A chance to use the DamoGO app as a marketing tool as it gives stores access to new customers and foot traffic and shows that the business cares about the environment and food waste

- Direct savings as a result of spending less on food waste management and disposal

- Access to data on food waste

User benefits:

- Savings of a minimum of 50 percent on delicious food

- Contribution to the reduction of both food waste and greenhouse gases

- Discovery of new restaurants they never would have tried at full price

Environmental benefits:

- Less food waste, which means lower greenhouse gas emissions

- Lower greenhouse gas emissions, which mean less harm done to the environment

Government benefits:

- Significant savings, as demonstrated by research showing that less food waste means less spent on waste management.

IMPLEMENTATION AND APPLICATION

Profit turnover at Sprout Vegan Restaurant

DamoGO services launched on the iOS and Android platforms on April 29, 2019. To test the feasibility of the project, we launched the platform for 15 stores in Seoul.

One restaurant that uses the service is Sprout Vegan Restaurant. Sprout makes a full menu of home-cooked-style meals. Sprout was founded in 2015 by a registered

FIGURE 6.3

Sprout profits with and without the DamoGO app in, US$

Surplus food without

Sprout 25 meals

Food cost $5 each	- $100
Labor cost $2.5 each	- $50
Total cost	**- $150**

-$150 + Food waste fees $20

Surplus food with

Sprout 25 meals

Regular price $5 each	- $100
DamoGO price (50% off)	+ $50
DamoGO commission of original price (25%)	- $12.50
Store extra profit	**+ $37.50**

Something that would have been thrown away now generates profit.

holistic nutritionist who wanted to promote a diet made with whole, natural food ingredients.

One problem Sprout owners faced every day since they launched was that they had to throw away 25–30 meals every Tuesday through Thursday. This happened because they offer their online delivery services on the weekend and Monday and are left with a handful of meals the day after, for numerous reasons, such as errors and canceled orders. As soon as Sprout partnered with DamoGO, its employees uploaded these items to the app and was able to connect with customers to rescue the food. The example in figure 6.3 shows the profit Sprout makes on 20 meals by partnering with DamoGO.

As of July 2019, Sprout had "rescued" 25 meals that otherwise would have been thrown away, generating US$60 in profits. Four food waste bags would have been purchased from the Seoul government (at $10 per bag) to dispose of this food.

Rescued food from the Indonesian Embassy in Seoul and the Seoul Central Mosque

DamoGO is not only a for-profit business; it also launched a social program (figure 6.4). From May 4 to June 5, 2019, Muslims in Seoul observed Ramadan. Both the Indonesian Embassy in Korea and the Seoul Central Mosque provided a free buffet to those who wanted to break their fast. Since both groups are uncertain how much food will be served, both places always cook extra, resulting in excess food.

The DamoGO team rescued the extra food and gave it to people in need in the surrounding areas by packing food into our custom-made container (figure 6.5). Over just two weekends, we rescued more than 450 meals.

Korean law permits food to be donated if it is given on or before the expiration date. Businesses that donate food are not liable for problems with the food if it was donated in fresh condition and was suitable to consume.

FIGURE 6.4
DamoGO collaborates with companies to rescue food

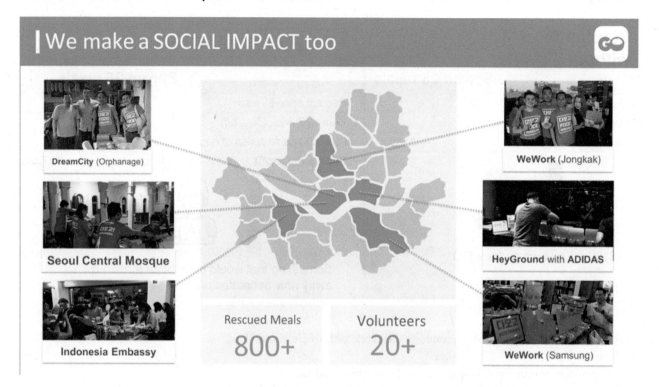

DEVELOPMENT PLAN AND MILESTONES

We will focus on well-known independently owned stores and restaurants at the beginning and then target larger chains and franchises after creating strong brand awareness (figure 6.6, panel a). After we raise seed funding in Q4 2019, we will have the funds to launch an aggressive marketing campaign to create awareness about the product. We will focus on sales, marketing, and branding, moving quickly. Our intent is to quickly and aggressively increase the market share, especially in countries of the Association of Southeast Asian Nations (ASEAN) (figure 6.6, panel b).

MILESTONES

2017–18

Citypreneurs Urban Innovation Challenge International Start-Up Competition Semifinalist

- DamoGO entered the Citypreneurs start-up competition only two weeks after our initial idea development, in September 2017. Even though we had been around for only two weeks, we were selected as a semifinalist among start-ups from all over the world.

Invitation to present at the MarkPlus Conference

- DamoGO was selected to give a presentation on sustainability and impact at the INA Forum at the MarkPlus Conference in Jakarta, one of Asia's largest marketing conferences, in December 2018. This opportunity gave us great exposure to Indonesian investors and potential partners and laid a strong foundation for our future expansion into the Indonesian market.

FIGURE 6.5

DamoGO with Seoul Central Mosque and the Indonesian Embassy in the Republic of Korea

Photos: DamoGO.

FIGURE 6.6

DamoGO's growth and scale following development plan

(a) Growth and Scale of DamoGO in Korea

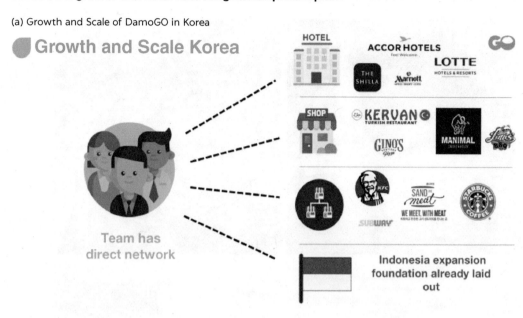

(b) Timeline for Growth

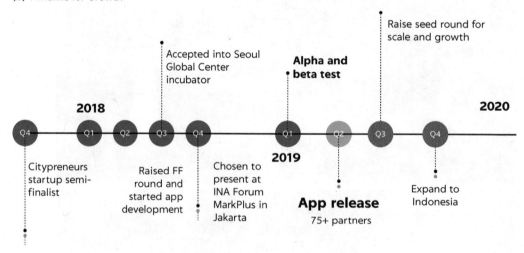

Note: FF = Friends and family round of financing.

2018–19

Finalist at the Indonesian Regional Investment Forum (RIF)

- Four hundred start-ups from around the world applied; DamoGO was a finalist selected to present at RIF, a yearly forum for start-ups and investment, in March 2019. Attendees and audience members include venture capital firms, angel investors, and government officials that are looking for start-ups that can be profitable, make an impact, and help solve government problems. DamoGO was connected with various venture capital and angel investors from the event.

Collaboration with Jakarta Smart City 2030

- At RIF in Indonesia, DamoGO was selected by the city of Jakarta to collaborate with the city to make it into a smart city and help reduce food waste there. We will be working with the city when we launch in Indonesia later in 2019.

Seoul Global Startup Center incubation program

- DamoGO applied and pitched at the city-funded Seoul Startup Global Center and was selected to be part of the incubation program in May 2019. Seoul believes in our vision.

Finalist at IFC D.Day at D.Camp

- DamoGO was selected as a finalist for D.Day with the International Finance Corporation (IFC) at D.Camp in March 2019. We were exposed to and met IFC executives as well as several venture capital firms, angel investors, and accelerators.

Top 40 Ashoka Changemakers Asia Region (CXC 2019)

- DamoGO's cofounder, Muhammad Farras, was selected as one of the top 10 Ashoka Changemakers in the Asia region for 2019.

Prototype, app development, and beta launch

- Our prototype design was completed in August 2018; app development began in October 2018. Our app was in beta testing as of May 2019 and was launched the third week in May.

COMPETITOR AND THREATS

DamoGO currently has only one direct competitor in Korea. Last Order launched its web application on July 21, 2018, in the Android app store. It was announced on July 30 that it had received investment from Danal, a Korean mobile payment company. Terms were undisclosed. The firm released its full app in November and had over 1,000 partners as of May 2019.

Although Last Order is positioning itself as an app to reduce food waste, it is actually more of a discount, or coupon, app. Partners give Last Order one or two regular menu items. The app uploads those menu items at the same time each day at around a 20 percent discount. Our research shows that a 20–30 percent discount is not enough to entice users to make a purchase and go to the store to pick it up. We also think that Last Order's business model is not sustainable. It charges each store US$30 per month to be listed on the app. Even with 1,000 stores, revenue would be only US$30,000 per month, which would barely cover payroll expenses. This could be part of Last Order's strategy to quickly sign on stores by taking only a monthly fee and not part of the stores' revenue. The team does not have the combination of food industry experience and network of food industry contacts that DamoGO's team has.

Overseas apps

Similar successful apps can be found in various countries (table 6.1). The biggest ones include Too Good to Go (United Kingdom), Karma (Sweden), Food for All (United States), and ResQ Club (Finland). Karma raised $12 million by August 2018 and $18 million by February 2019; Too Good to Go raised $6.8 million (total

TABLE 6.1 **Companies around the world that are similar to DamoGO**

UNITED KINGDOM	DENMARK	UNITED STATES	SWEDEN	FRANCE	NETHERLANDS	GERMANY
TGTG	TGTG	Food for All	Karma	TGTG	TGTG	TGTG
Karma	YourLocal	GoMKT	ResQClub	OptiMiam	ResQClub	ResQClub
UGO Fresh	RedMaden	MOGO			NoFoodWasted	
	Wefood	PareUP				
	Stop Madspild					

Note: TGTG = Too Good to Go.

$20.4 million by February 2019) for expansion across Europe (Crunchbase 2019). These apps could target Korea by opening local offices. However, these businesses have been around less than three years. Their current focus is growth in Europe.

Korean discount apps

Various apps in Korea focus on discounted products. Some of them include food items. Thirty Mall, Sale Factory, and Convenience Store 1+1 do not focus on perishable food but instead sell canned food, chips, snacks, candy, and health products. T-Mon and Coupang do not focus on perishable food. Some of these apps are not platforms for stores to sell their goods directly; instead, they take possession of inventory and resell expiring products.

CONCLUSIONS

We knew that other entrepreneurs might offer a similar app to DamoGO's. We wanted to be the first mover and had plans to defend from competitors entering the market. We are not first because of Last Order, but we still have many advantages over them. Korea has room for more than one player in this field—even three or four. Delivery apps in Korea have at least five or six main players—such as Baemin, YoGiYo, Baedal Tong, Ding Dong, and Food Fly. On-demand hotel or motel reservations have Yeogi Uh-Tae, Ya Nol Ja, Yeogi Ya, and others. Rideshare services include Uber Korea, Kakao Taxi, and others.

In the food waste app space around the world, many countries have more than one player; in some cases, there are up to five competing start-ups. Becoming the market leader comes down to sales, marketing, and branding. We at DamoGO plan to be very aggressive in all three funcitons right from the beginning. After initial success and rapid growth, we plan to immediately enter Southeast Asia, which has much larger markets than Korea. We have a long-term vision of being far and away the market leader in Asia.

DAMOGO'S FUTURE

DamoGO has already been making noise in Indonesia. A launch in the world's fourth most populous country will happen with a second round of seed funding. Indonesia's economy is growing; there is immense opportunity for a start-up like ours to do big things there (figure 6.7). We have already developed deep and strong contacts and connections there and have been featured in various media

FIGURE 6.7

DamoGO's future expansion into Indonesia

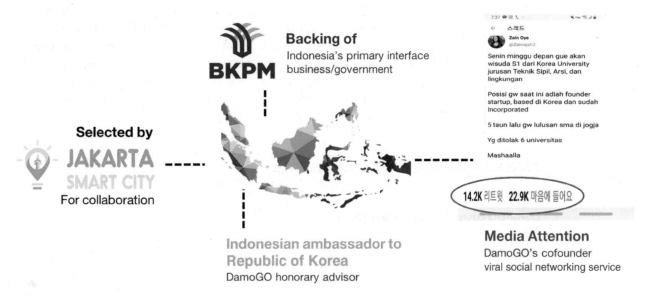

FIGURE 6.8

DamoGO market potential in the Republic of Korea and members of the Association of Southeast Asian Nations

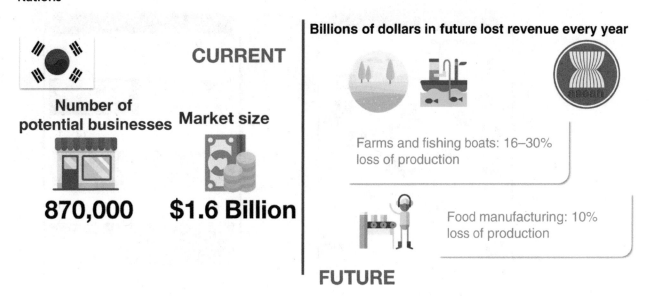

outlets. We are now part of Jakarta Smart City and will collaborate with the city when we launch there. We are also a part of BKPM, the Indonesian Investment Coordinating Board and a powerful entity in the country. It will be helping us expand in Indonesia. Indonesia's ambassador to Korea, Umar Hadi, will help us become even stronger and help us address the country's food waste problem. After expansion to Indonesia, we have our sights on the other members of ASEAN.

Our team's food industry experience and research have allowed DamoGO to come up with several future add-ons and revenue-generating ideas. These future revenue streams will also have significant positive social and environmental impacts. Our team's experience and future add-ons will keep DamoGO one step ahead of any competition (figure 6.8).

Korea has 870,000 restaurants, cafés, and bakeries. If each store sells four items a day at an average priceof US$4 an item, the market is worth US$1.6 billion.

According to the Food and Agriculture Organization of the United Nations (Gustavsson and others 2011), up to 30 percent of losses in farming and fishing every year are due to overproduction, and about 10 percent of food is lost in the food manufacturing sector. Although DamoGO currently operates in the business-to-consumer sector, in the future we want to reduce food waste in the business-to-business sector as well.

ANNEX 6A. DAMOGO APP SCREENSHOTS

FIGURE 6A.1

DamoGO customer app screenshots

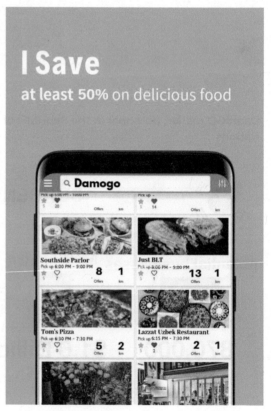

FIGURE 6A.1, *continued*

Buy
delicious items right on the app

Go
Pick up
at the store during their pick up
hours and show QR code receipt

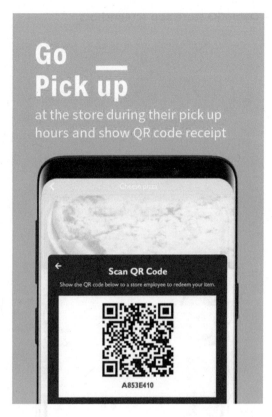

Follow
your favorite stores to receive
immediate notifications

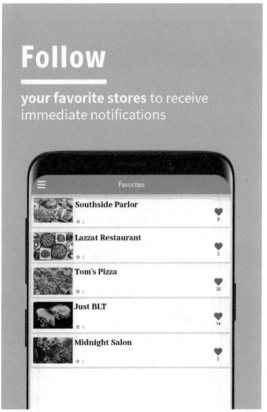

FIGURE 6A.2

DamoGO store app screenshots

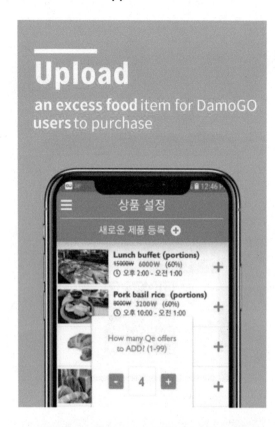

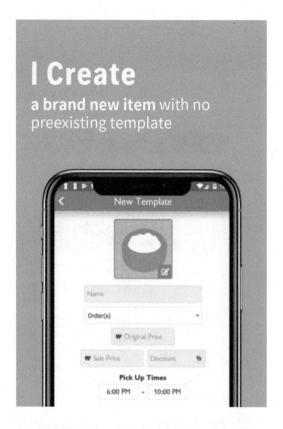

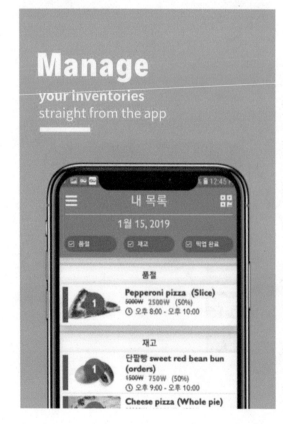

ANNEX 6B. MEDIA COVERAGE

Bella, Annisa. 2018. "DamoGO: Create Taste, Not Waste." Marketeers, December 5. http://marketeers.com/damogo-create-taste-not-waste/.

Chung, Jeannie. 2019. "DamoGO Rescues Delicious Food and Reduces Waste." Seoul Global Startup Center. May 15. http://seoulgsc.com/damogo-rescues-delicious-food-and-reduces-waste/.

Purwadhika Connect. 2018. "Cerita Sukses Farras, Anak Muda Indonesia Yang Membuat Startup di Korea." December 5. https://medium.com/purwadhikaconnect/cerita-sukses-farras-anak-muda-indonesia-yang-membuat-startup-di-korea-7e088f7ffc4a.

Rianta, Surya. 2019. "Kisah Farras Membangun Startup di Negeri Orang." *Bisnis Indonesia*, March 18. https://teknologi.bisnis.com/read/20190318/266/901051/kisah-farras-membangun-startup-di-negeri-orang.

NOTE

This project has been supported by the Indonesia Investment Promotion Center (BKPM) in Seoul, the Seoul Metropolitan Government, the Seoul Global Startup Center Batch 4, and the Jakarta Smart City 2030 program in Indonesia.

REFERENCES

Carrington, Damian. 2018. "One in Three Fish Caught Never Makes It to the Plate—UN Report." *Guardian*, July 9. https://www.theguardian.com/environment/2018/jul/09/one-in-three-fish-caught-never-makes-it-to-the-plate-un-report

Flanders Investment & Trade Seoul. 2014. "A Snapshot of the Bakery Industry in South Korea." Flanders Investment & Trade market survey, Seoul, August.

Gustavsson, Jenny, Christel Cederberg, Ulf Sonesson, Robert van Otterdijk, and Alexandre Meybeck. 2011. *Global Food Losses and Food Waste: Extent, Causes, and Prevention.* Food and Agriculture Organization of the United Nations, Rome.

Jung, Min-hee. 2016. "Single-Person Households Creating New Trend of Consumption." *Business Korea*, January 7.

Ministry of Environment. 2018. "Reducing Food Waste! The Great Action to Save the Earth." Consumer guide, Seoul. http://me.go.kr/home/file/readDownloadFile.do;jsessionid=8j43EcF1D3nr886xIrDyAbbA.mehome2?fileId=105596&fileSeq=2.

Seo, H. 2018. "7 Out of 10 Small Businesses 'Unable to Cope with Minimum Wage Hike.'" *Korea Bizwire*, July 23.

Statista. 2016. "Number of General Restaurants in South Korea from 2008 to 2017 (in thousands)." https://www.statista.com/statistics/786574/south-korea-general-restaurant-number/.

Statistics Korea. 2018. 경기도 안산시 음식물쓰레기납부필증가격정보. https://www.data.go.kr/dataset/15028497/fileData.do.

Verrill, Courtney. 2016. "American Restaurants Are Wasting an Incredible Amount of Food—Here's Proof." *Business Insider,* May 17. https://www.businessinsider.com/solving-food-waste-in-americas-restaurants-2016-5.

ADDITIONAL READING

Gavilan, Ignacio, and Brian Lipinski. 2017. "Call to Action to Standardize Food Date Labels Worldwide by 2020." Consumer Goods Forum. https://champions123.org/wp-content/uploads/2017/09/champions-123-call-to-action-to-standardize-food-date-labels-worldwide-by-2020.pdf.

Ministry of Environment, Republic of Korea. 2016. *Food Waste in Korea Report 2016*.

World Business Council for Sustainable Development. 2017. "Private Sector Food Producers Line Up Behind First Ever Global Initiative to Cut Food Losses." September 20. https://www.wbcsd.org/Programs/Food-Land-Water/Food-Land-Use/Climate-Smart-Agriculture/News/first-ever-global-initiative-to-cut-food-losses.

7 Fresh Water and Ice Solution for Fishing Communities on Remote Islands of Indonesia

SHANA FATINA, *Founder and CEO*

ATIEK PUSPA FADHILAH, *Cofounder*

FAKHRI GUNIAR, *Project officer*

ABSTRACT Komodo Water (KW), established in 2010, is a social enterprise that provides fresh water and ice blocks for Papagarang Island and surrounding small islands in Komodo National Park in Indonesia. KW is working to improve access to clean water and fresh fish supplies through a better cold preservation chain. Our key activities are producing fresh water and ice blocks from the brackish water on the island. The water is treated using a reverse-osmosis system, with solar energy as the power source. By using our ice blocks, our customers can compete fairly in providing fresh fish to premium markets. KW partners with a village-owned company and small grocery kiosks to distribute the products through a profit-sharing scheme. The setup is important because Indonesia consists of small islands that rely heavily on diesel generators and that struggle to develop their economic activities. Our business model in providing water and ice blocks will be replicable in other small islands.

Fishing communities in Komodo National Park, a tourist destination, are struggling to avoid becoming a potential threat to conservation and practice sustainable fishing inside the park. With the UN Sustainable Development Goals (SDGs) in mind, the KW mission is to bring a solution for ensuring the availability and sustainable management of water (SDG 6) by promoting the use of sustainable energy (SDG 7) and reducing waste generation (SDG 12), as well as protecting the marine ecosystem (SDG 14) and creating opportunities for good and decent jobs and secure livelihoods (SDG 8).

Team Komodo Water.

FIGURE 7.1

Economic situation in fishing communities of Komodo National Park

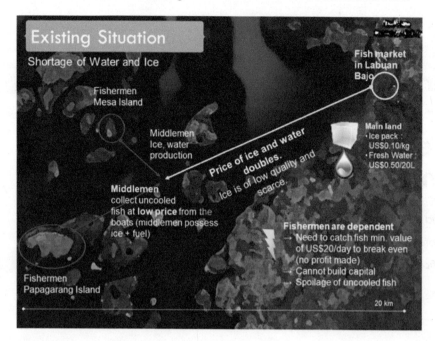

Source: GIZ Indonesia.

PROBLEM AND CONTEXT

The project is located on Papagarang Island, in the Komodo National Park, in Indonesia, where freshwater supplies and rainfall have become scarce, forcing fishers to fish farther away. Inadequate fresh water and the 12-hour energy supply available from diesel generators impede their use of proper cooling technology for their fish. These factors cause up to 50 percent of their catches to be sold as salted fish, at a significantly lower price than fresh fish. A schematic explanation of the island situation is shown in figure 7.1.

To meet the need for fresh water and ice packs, existing suppliers bring ice by a two-hour boat trip from Labuan Bajo (figure 7.2). The ice packs are not durable for long trips, during which fishers seek fish away from the conservation area. The use of plastic ice packs has resulted in severe plastic litter problems in the seascape. The plastic problem in Indonesia has caught international attention and generated headlines (Makur 2017).

Although the islands are in a conservation area, diesel generators are the most common technology providing electricity in the national park and its surroundings. The use of diesel fuel, with its residual substances and noise, will harm the natural ecosystem.

FIGURE 7.2

Salted fish and plastic ice packs in daily fishing activities

Photos: Komodo Water.

These challenges are apparent in other small islands in Indonesia as well as in other archipelagic countries. The lack of energy, fresh water, and ice for fishers is interdependent.

Once this initiative is proved to be sustainable, many islands with similar characteristics will be eager to adopt the business model. Most of the initiatives in the islands at the moment are grant programs from the Indonesian government or institutions managed by informal groups that are not yet applying good management practices. They have led most of the previous programs to become abandoned and fail just after delivery to the communities.

Our mission is to develop an end-to-end sustainable solution, by adopting a community-driven social entrepreneurial approach. A proven social business in this area can be one of the solutions to drive economic development in small islands and coastal communities. The program should include the development of a community management organization, which will make sure the program is sustainable. It will directly contribute to the SDGs by ensuring the availability and sustainable management of water, promoting uses of sustainable energy, and reducing waste generation. Our initiative will also have positive effects on the preservation of the marine ecosystem and create opportunities for jobs and better livelihoods.

SOLUTION

Better product, more sustainable management

KW focuses on the provision of fresh water and ice blocks for fishers by using clean technology. KW uses efficient reverse-osmosis machines and ice-block machines powered by solar energy. In 2019, we switched our diesel-powered reverse-osmosis machine to a 100 percent solar-powered machine. The ice-block machine will use a natural refrigerant that causes minimum harm to the environment. This design makes it 100 percent free of greenhouse gas emissions. We purify brackish water with total dissolved solids (TDS) of 9,000 parts per million (ppm) into drinking water with TDS 11–13 ppm, certified by the National Health Department, and sell it in refillable 20-liter jerry cans. The ice-block dimensions (10 kilograms/block) are bigger and more flexible to use and store than existing ice supplies (1-kilogram ice packs). Fishers do not need to buy the individually wrapped smaller packages, instead placing the ice directly into their own storage boxes. Not only fishers but also their customers can store the ice blocks longer than before, because they can crush them to store their fish or for any purpose. The technology enables fishers to sail farther, searching for better fish and avoiding the conservation area.

The machines are manufactured by prominent companies in refrigeration, desalination, and solar energy. We plan to sell the ice blocks for Rp 15,000/block and Rp 15,000/20 liters of drinking water. These prices are competitive with existing suppliers who have to bring ice packs and water from Labuan Bajo by boat on a two-hour trip.

The tourism industry is growing in and near Komodo National Park (Remmer 2017). Tourism will drive more consumption of fresh fish. Availability of ice blocks will mitigate the risk of overfishing in areas surrounding the park. We target the residents of Komodo National Park, especially in Papagarang, Mesa, and other surrounding small islands, who work as fishers and fish sellers. Tourist boats and food stalls are also potential customers. Customers can pick up ice and fresh water or order them via our resellers.

Benefits to surrounding communities

After conducting a focus group discussion in a village with the village administration and community, we will formulate a mechanism that can benefit community members. Each village in Indonesia is entitled to have a village-owned company conduct business that benefits the community. These community-based businesses are called *Badan Usaha Milik Desa* (BUMDes). BUMDes will be the main distributors for our products, selling the products to agents and kiosks on other islands (see figure 7.3). We will create opportunities for small kiosks in the surrounding islands to be the resellers. This partnership was proposed by the village head and the community during a focus group discussion. As distributors, they will purchase at a price that will enable them to make a business of it.

On top of our business activities, we frequently conduct community development activities on trash management, tourism, and education. We connect with stakeholders from outside the area to familiarize them with challenges on the island and implement solutions.

A maintenance contract will be signed by KW and the technology providers to sustain the machine operation and handle routine maintenance. We will develop an integrated community management program, including designing a customized organization to run the operation, which will enable villagers to manage and operate the machine. We will provide simple, instructions, divide the work among workflow stations, and rotate nonpermanent workers to increase their ownership in the daily operation (see figure 7.4).

We also teach local people basic technical skills to maintain the machine. Success will be determined by the number of households that can access fresh water from our services as well as the income of the fishers who use our ice blocks. Rising income is expected, because their catches will stay fresh when they arrive at market, allowing them to earn higher prices for their fresh fish (up to three times the price of salted fish).

BUSINESS MODEL

The business model for KW also incorporates the social and environmental costs of the business activities (see figure 7.5). In conducting our business activities, we will optimize the social and environmental benefits of the project while minimizing the costs.

FIGURE 7.3

Komodo Water's business process

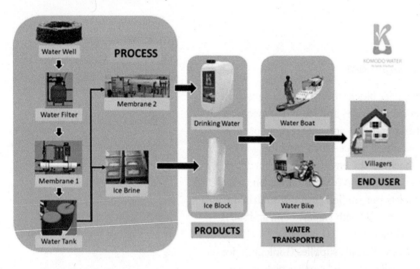

Source: Komodo Water.

FIGURE 7.4

Komodo Water's cooperation scheme with village BUMDes

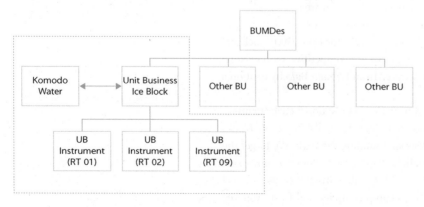

Note: BUMDes = *Badan Usaha Milik Desa* (community-based business); BU = business unit; RT = *Rukun Tetangga* (smallest government unit); UB = unit business.

FIGURE 7.5

Komodo Water's business model

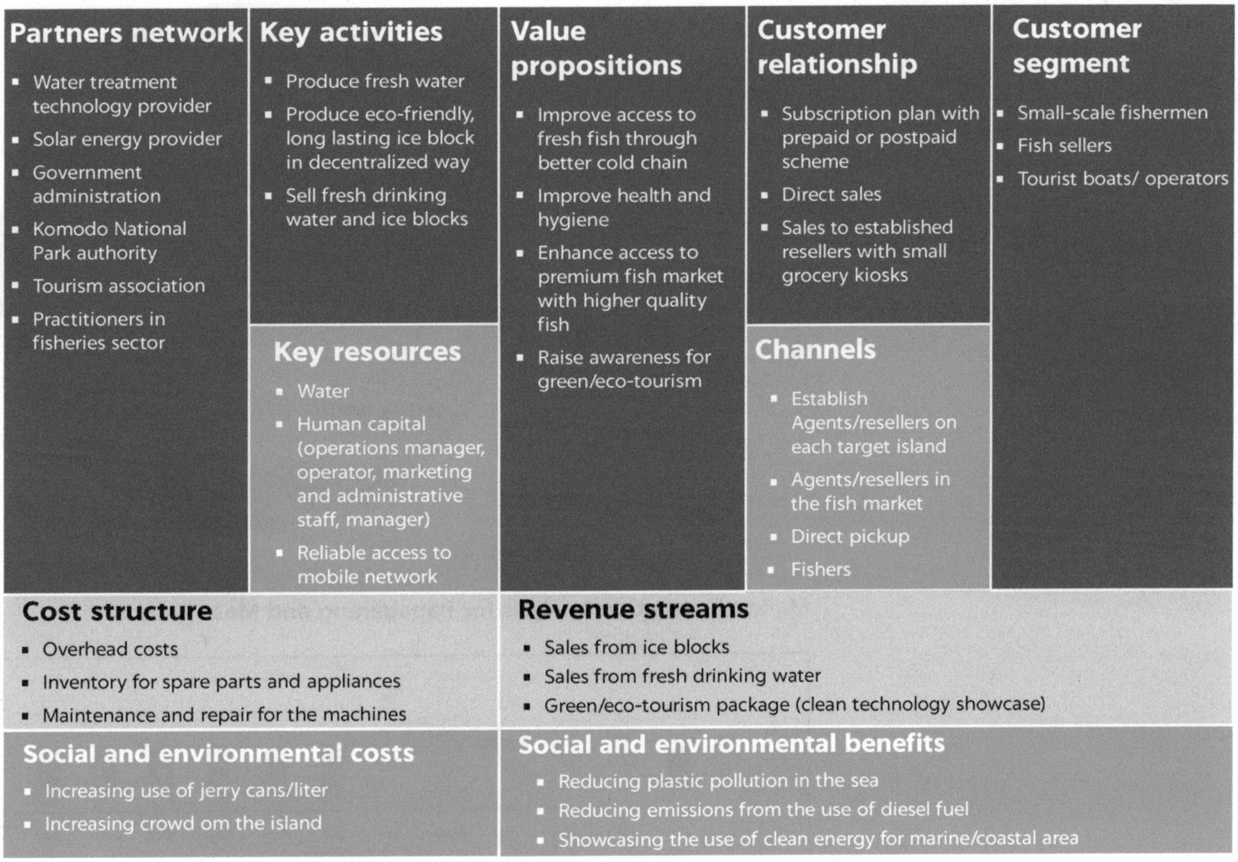

Partners network	Key activities	Value propositions	Customer relationship	Customer segment
• Water treatment technology provider • Solar energy provider • Government administration • Komodo National Park authority • Tourism association • Practitioners in fisheries sector	• Produce fresh water • Produce eco-friendly, long lasting ice block in decentralized way • Sell fresh drinking water and ice blocks	• Improve access to fresh fish through better cold chain • Improve health and hygiene • Enhance access to premium fish market with higher quality fish • Raise awareness for green/eco-tourism	• Subscription plan with prepaid or postpaid scheme • Direct sales • Sales to established resellers with small grocery kiosks	• Small-scale fishermen • Fish sellers • Tourist boats/ operators
	Key resources • Water • Human capital (operations manager, operator, marketing and administrative staff, manager) • Reliable access to mobile network		**Channels** • Establish Agents/resellers on each target island • Agents/resellers in the fish market • Direct pickup • Fishers	

Cost structure
- Overhead costs
- Inventory for spare parts and appliances
- Maintenance and repair for the machines

Revenue streams
- Sales from ice blocks
- Sales from fresh drinking water
- Green/eco-tourism package (clean technology showcase)

Social and environmental costs
- Increasing use of jerry cans/liter
- Increasing crowd om the island

Social and environmental benefits
- Reducing plastic pollution in the sea
- Reducing emissions from the use of diesel fuel
- Showcasing the use of clean energy for marine/coastal area

KW offers a reliable supply of drinking water and ice blocks to fishers and coastal communities. By using our ice blocks product, customers can keep their catches fresh and will have more open access to the premium fish market in Labuan Bajo. In the meantime, our fresh drinking water provides a significant competitive advantage over the current water supply. Our water and ice-block products offer healthier and cleaner consumables than the alternatives.

TARGET MARKET

Our primary target market is the residents of islands around the Komodo area, about 2,800 households, which generate demand for 30,000 gallons of water and 192,000 kilograms of ice per year. Our market research shows that there is a daily demand of 6.5 tons of ice during the peak season and 3.1 tons of ice during the low season (see figure 7.6). We calculate that our daily production of one-ton ice blocks can be absorbed by the market.

During market research, we mapped the demand pattern of our main potential customers, particularly on two major islands for fishers: Papagarang and Mesa Islands. As seen in figure 7.7, the main demand for ice blocks comes from fishers in Mesa Islands, especially during February to June.

FIGURE 7.6

Market share analysis of households (HH) and ice demand

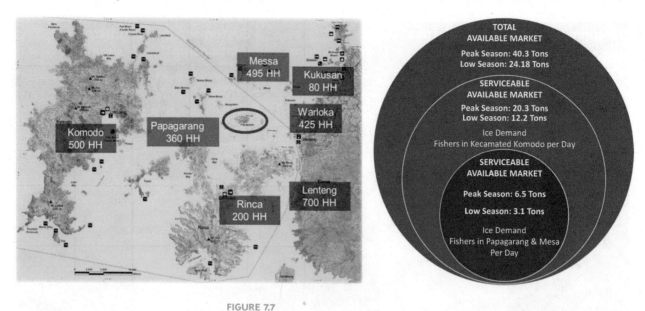

FIGURE 7.7

Market fluctuation analysis for Papagarang and Mesa Islands

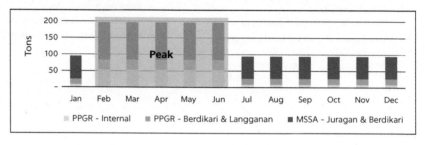

Source: Komodo Water.

Note: Berdikari = independent fishers; Juragan = fisher's bosses; Langganan = dependent fishers; PPGR = Papagarang; MSSA = Mesa Islands.

COMPETITOR ANALYSIS

Existing suppliers of fresh water and ice packs deliver their supplies by a two-hour boat trip to Labuan Bajo. Usually, fishers obtain their ice packs in the morning, when they also sell their fish, and then use the ice in the evening. Often, the ice packs have already melted when the fishers set sail. The ice packs last for only a one-day trip, are insufficient for long trips, and cost about 6 percent more to produce than KW ice blocks. The existing system of ice packs also causes severe plastic waste in the sea. Current ice pack producers use household freezers; factory-size producers can have 20 household-size freezers for daily production (see figure 7.8).

KW's use of solar energy will compete with the current use of diesel generators, which harm the natural ecosystem with residual substances and noise. The KW system is free of greenhouse gas emissions.

Government grant projects have failed because they were not followed up with proper management. Trainings were usually too short, and the projects usually selected the wrong person as the formal representative of the village. We have striven to establish a social-business model to serve the basic needs of communities. We will develop the business together with the community from the beginning, formalizing the partnership in the form of BUMDes as the management organization.

FIGURE 7.8

Komodo Water's clean technology

a. Current practice on Buru Island using diesel fuel

b. Common method at Labuan Bajo using household freezers to make ice packs

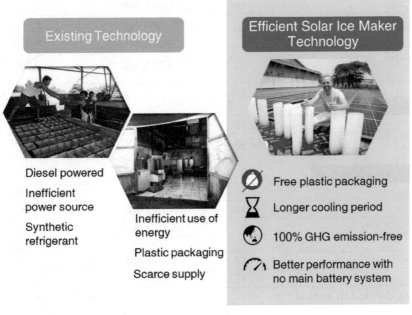

Photos: Komodo Water.
Note: GHG = greenhouse gases.

TECHNOLOGY PARTNERS

The solar ice maker technology has been developed through a technology transfer scheme between the German and Indonesian public and private sectors. Design and manufacturing instructions are prepared by German institutions; manufacturing until implementation activities is conducted by Indonesian institutions.

The first version of this technology is being tested through the scheme, with KW serving as the research partner. KW scales up implementation of the machine with a sound business scheme, developed on the basis of our presence and experience in the area. Desalination is supported through a collaboration with French private institutions, for both the renewable power and the water desalination systems. For the first year of operation, the technology providers have committed to closely monitor the operation and provide necessary supports.

FINANCIAL PROJECTION

KW's revenue comes from two products: 10-kilogram ice blocks and 20-liter jerry cans of drinking water. Annually, we will generate about US$66,000 (table 7.1) from both products, based on sales of 240 tons of ice blocks and 1,080 cubic meters of drinking water when production runs at full capacity, which we expect will take three years. We forecast sales to reach 40 percent of potential in the first year, 80 percent in the second year, and 100 percent in the third year (see figure 7.9).

Payback will be reached in the fourth year to cover the investment of US$55,000 (see figure 7.10). The amount is dominated by installations, civil works, and engineering services. The development cost to build a new solar-powered ice machine is excluded from this calculation. Operational costs of US$25,000 a year will cover

TABLE 7.1. Financial analysis

INVESTMENT	Volume	Amount [Rp]	Amount [US$]
Installation of ice maker		200,000,000	14,085
Installation of water desalination		115,000,000	50,000
Installation of power system		200,000,000	14,085
Market research		85,000,000	5,986
Civil works		200,000,000	14,085
Working capital (3 months of operational expenses + sales strategy)		53,781,900	3,787
INCOME			
Revenue from ice block	24,278	485,568,000	34,195
Revenue from water	41,861.00	455,027,600	32,044
OPERATIONAL EXPENSES			
Fresh water	12	36,417,600	2,565
Salt	12	16,560,000	1,166
Salaries		153,250,000	10,792
Consumables power		500,000	35
Consumables ice machine	12	3,600,000	254
Overhead costs	12	4,800,000	338
Component replacement (ice machine), divided to annual			2,565
Batteries			–
Evaporator			–
Pumps			–
Stirrer			–
Bins			–
Consumables and component replacement (water)			
Filters and consumables		3,150,000	222
Chemical material		1,050,000	74
Membrane reverse osmosis		1,200,000	85

drinking water and salt supply for ice block production; component replacement; and consumables such as water filters, salaries, and overhead costs. For ice production, we will buy water from our own water production at 30 percent of its retail price. We amortize the machines based on their lifetime and 1 percent of income tax for small to medium enterprises in Indonesia. Each component and consumable has a different replacement schedule on which we based our maintenance schedule.

CHANGES

Positive effect of Komodo water for people

- Each kilogram of ice block used will increase the value of fish sold by fishers by US$0.50 per kilogram, generating additional income for traditional fishers of about US$98,000 annually.

- Onsite water availability will reduce dependence on the costly water supply from the mainland, enabling local people to cut costs for family water consumption by up to 40 percent annually.

- The fresh water will improve the health of local people, because it will replace water products that are untreated and unhealthy for consumption and have caused severe infections.

FIGURE 7.9
Five-year sales projections

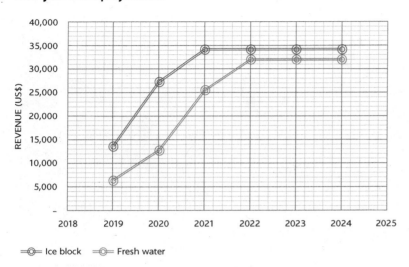

-○- Ice block   -○- Fresh water

FIGURE 7.10
Cumulative cashflow for 10 years

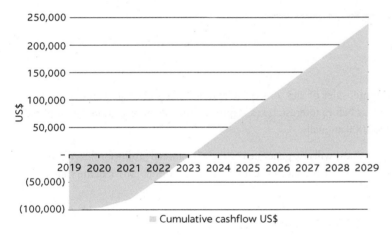

▩ Cumulative cashflow US$

Positive effect of Komodo water for the planet

- Producing water and ice blocks in the Papagarang Island will reduce occurrences of oil spills and fuel wasted in the ocean, because buying fresh water and ice packs in Labuan Bajo requires intensive boat use to transport them.

- Our solar-powered reverse-osmosis machine and ice maker produce fresh water and ice blocks without any emissions or pollution. The machines use 30 kWh of solar power, reducing fossil fuel consumption by 14,400 liters annually.

- Ice blocks without plastic wrap will replace the existing ice packs, reducing plastic litter in the marine conservation area. By selling 1,000 kilograms of ice in block form daily, we will eliminate the use of 1,000 plastic packs per day.

- The use of ice blocks helps fishers to fish longer. Fishers be able to reach more fishing areas and thus will fish in a larger fishing area, reducing stress inside Komodo National Park (see figure 7.11). Fishers will catch higher-quality fish, raising their income.

FIGURE 7.11

Fishing zone in Komodo National Park

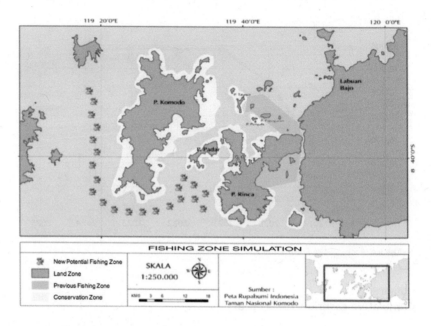

Source: Komodo National Park Authority.

Profit

- We target sales of 245 tons of ice and 840 liters of fresh water annually. Our earnings before interest, taxes, depreciation, and amortization are projected at US$73,000 annually.

- The business will also generate US$9,200 in annual profits for the village-owned enterprises. This profit can be used for further development of the village.

DEVELOPMENT PLAN

Progress to date

After succeeding in the first phase on fresh water supply, KW is now developing the second phase for ice block supply. We have conducted market research to identify the social structures of the society and determine the potential market in the area. We also have demonstrated the product in a test using a simple prototype that we built (see figure 7.12).

KW has recruited new personnel and reorganized our team to support the implementation plan (see table 7.2). Our team consists of a strong, solid combination of young, enthusiastic entrepreneurs and experienced entrepreneurs, academicians, community leaders, and technology innovators who share the same vision and commitment to increase the potential of remote coastal areas in Indonesia and worldwide.

We have updated our working permit from the villages and national park authorities and established a website (http://www.komodowater.org/) to reach wider audiences. We have finished drilling a well and designed the layout for machine installation in our factory on Papagarang Island (see figure 7.13).

FIGURE 7.12
Market research study

Photos: Komodo Water.

TABLE 7.2 **Team members**

POSITION	NAME
Founder & CEO	Shana Fatina
Cofounders	Chandra Novrizal, Atiek Puspa
Project Officer	Fakhri Guniar
Head of Production	Yohanes Ance
Head of Distribution	Jossy Raung
Community Manager	Basir Bochriel
Finance & Admin	Sensi Robert
Key Technology Partner	
Project Manager of Solar Ice Maker	Frank Stegmueller (GIZ)

FIGURE 7.13

Construction and machine installation for factory on Papagarang Island

Photos: Komodo Water.

MILESTONES

2019

We install the ice maker machine in Papagarang and operate it to validate the business model for replication. Our machine is finalized for transport and will be ready to be delivered by mid-2019. We focus on training local operators and village-owned enterprises and setting a standard operational procedure to regularly operate and be ready to replicate the projects at other potential sites (see figures 7.14 and 7.15).

2020–21

We plan to penetrate the market, which consists of more than 2,760 fisher families, 300 fishing boats, and 350 tourist boats that need ice blocks and water for daily operation. The current market size is up to 10 tons of ice a day and up to 100,000 liters of water a day.

We will operate and evaluate the operation annually. Using the findings, we will improve and replicate the pilot in other areas nationwide, with lower cost of production. We will also develop the system to remotely monitor project progress.

FIGURE 7.14

Timeline for Komodo Water

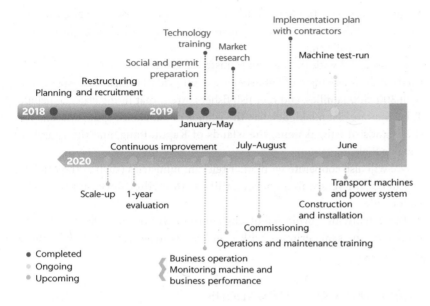

FIGURE 7.15

Milestones

2021–23

We have identified at least three islands that need fresh water and ice blocks and will start the initiation plan to replicate the project there.

SCALING UP

There are approximately 6,000 inhabited islands in Indonesia. The problems that we tackle in this initiative are apparent in most of the small islands, which will be our target for scaling up.

As discussed with Indonesia's Ministry of Fishery, our solution will fit the needs of the following types of fisher areas: off-grid islands, middle-size islands with 300–500 families, and reef-fish fishers. Areas that fit the criteria include- Takabonerate, Saumlaki, Selayar, the islands of Sapeken-Sapudi-Masalembu, the islands of Pangakajene, the islands of Kapoposang, and the islands of Padaido Biak.

We will also cooperate with other relevant ministries (such as the Ministry of Energy for renewable energy utilities) to further develop the project nationwide.

For worldwide development, the solution will be suitable for any locations with the same criteria, with adjustments to reflect social and cultural differences.

CHALLENGES AND MITIGATIONS

KW faces challenges in the preparation and execution of its business activities. In the preparation phase, we need to renovate the workshop and mobilize, install, integrate, and commission all the machinery. We anticipate the following significant challenges:

- Operating the first generation of solar-powered ice machines, which will require assistance from experts

- Educating the village-owned company to conduct good business management such as transparency, effective and efficient workflow, staffing, customer service, marketing and sales, and so on

- Hiring competent local staff to operate and maintain the machine, because the island community is not used to routine tasks and is highly influenced by the culture of fishers who have more autonomy

- Balancing expectations from the local community to instantly benefit from our business initiatives

- Getting our first loyal customers.

We may face unexpected faults or disruptions in operation and maintenance (O&M). We will mitigate these risks by providing an instruction manual in the local language for operators and training from manufacturers and contractors, and, in the first few years of operation, creating suitable O&M terms and warranty, so contractors and suppliers, are still responsible for unidentified technology problems.

KW will develop an integrated community management program to train villagers in managing and operating the machine. Our plan is to make simple, translated instructions and divided workflow stations, as well as rotate nonpermanent workers to increase their ownership in the daily operation.

We mapped our anticipated risks and mitigation measures (table 7.3).

TABLE 7.3 **Possible risks and strategies for mitigating them**

PRIORITY	TYPE OF RISK	CATEGORY	LIKELIHOOD	SEVERITY	MITIGATION PLAN
1	Capital structure: Investments are not fully covered	Compliance	Rare	High	• Find more funders by generating various investment packages. • Construct and install.
2	Regulatory: • Restricted area for business in the national park • Restricted area for buildings • Expanded restricted area for fishing	Compliance	Unlikely	High	• Maintain good relationship with the authorities. • Demonstrate impact to stakeholders • Align with local economic development plan. • Expand sales points to tourists and restaurants.
3	Market dynamics: Competition	Strategic	Possible	Moderate	• Conduct thorough market research. • Engage in product innovation. • Diversify pricing. • Diversify payment method.
	Price competition risk				• Divide payment value into smaller but more frequent amounts, through bundling or membership programs.
4	Hazards: Earthquake and tsunami	Operational	Possible	Moderate	• Use earthquake-proof building. • Purchase insurance.
5	Market practice: Failed prepaid method	Compliance	Possible	Minor	• Use other payment method.
6	Currency fluctuation	Strategic	Possible	Minimal	• Include sufficient allowance in the financial model. • Use complementary local spare parts.
7	Liquidity: • Payment default	Financial	Likely	Major	• Innovate with payment schemes. • Divide the risk by partnering with village-owned company and resellers.
	• Seasonality				• Adopt cashflow management. • Hire extra staff in high season.
8	Physical assets: • Long downtime	Operational	Likely	Minor	• Regularly conduct operation and maintenance as required in the instruction manual and guide. • Agree to support the operation of the machine. • Commission experts.
	- Low machine reliability	Operational	Likely	Major	

REFERENCES

Makur, Markus. 2017. "Labuan Bajo Faces Challenges with Rising Tourism." *Jakarta Post*, Sept. 7. https://www.thejakartapost.com/travel/2017/09/07/labuan-bajo-faces-challenges-with -rising-tourism.html.

Remmer, Stefanie. 2017. *Tourism Impacts in Labuan Bajo*. WISATA, Tourism Development for Selected Destinations in Indonesia. https://www.swisscontact.org/fileadmin/user_upload /HEAD_OFFICE/Pictures/Tourismus_Landing_page/Labuan_Bajo_Impact_Assessment.pdf.

ADDITIONAL READING

Axaopoulos, P. J., and M. P. Theodoridis. 2009. "Design and Experimental Performance of a PV Ice Maker without Battery." *Solar Energy* 83 (March).

ILK Dresden. 2014. "Elaboration of a Concept for the PV Energy Supply of Block Ice Machines on Buru Island (Indonesia)." GIZ (German Agency for International Cooperation), October.

Isaak, David. 1980. "Solar Icemakers for Rural Development: Technical Prospects." Energy for Rural Department Program Report (inter-country program with support from U.S. Agency for International Development), September.

Promotion of Least Cost Renewables in Indonesia (LCORE-INDO). 2014. "Assessments and Optimisation Measures in an Ice Block Factory in Buru Island." GIZ (German Agency for International Cooperation), October.

Promotion of Least Cost Renewables in Indonesia (LCORE-INDO). 2015. "Case Study: Solar Ice Making. Energy Efficiency and Solar PV Concepts." GIZ (German Agency for International Cooperation), January.

Pusat Pengendalian Pembangunan Ekoregion Bali dan Nusa Tenggara. 2018. "Daya Dukung Wisata Taman Nasional Komodo." Ministry of Forestry and Environment, December.

Friendly Doctor: Building Technology-Driven Bridges between MSM/LGBTI Individuals and Public Health Institutions

TEAM COMMUNITY HEALTH LEADERS

TYMUR LEVCHUK, *Executive director of NGO Fulcrum UA*

YANA TOVPEKO, *Communications manager of NGO Fulcrum UA*

ROMAN IVASIY, *Coordinator of health direction of NGO Fulcrum UA*

MARYNA DIDENKO, *Psychologist of NGO Fulcrum UA*

ABSTRACT Friendly Doctor, an online peer-driven intervention system, is an effective model for screening for human immunodeficiency virus (HIV) among men who have sex with men (MSM) and lesbian, gay, bisexual, transexual, and intersexual (LGBTI) individuals in Ukraine. It consists of a website (friendly-doctor.org) on which an individual can register and get an appointment for HIV screening in a safe and convenient environment. In the case of a positive result, a doctor works with the individual. Screening offices are located separately from nongovernmental organizations and medical facilities, guaranteeing clients' full anonymity. The doctor who conducts the screening is an employee of an AIDS center. The online portal allows appointments, the opportunity to receive treatment regimens and discuss them with a doctor online, a record of the treatment history, and reminders to take medication and get medical examinations. A mobile application (Friendly Doc) makes it easy to make appointments with doctors. The app is available for iOS and Android.

Footmo Kit: Developing a Low-Cost, Handheld Device for Detecting Foot and Mouth Disease in Livestock in Hard-to-Reach and Underserved Areas

TEAM FOOTMO KIT

MUSHUSHA RICHARD, *CEO, Obama fellow, innovator, entrepreneur, founder and CEO of Footmo Kit, and cofounder of Whole Mentorship Organization Limited*

MISEARCH LUMIISA, *Sensor designer*

KICONCHO BENADINE, *Veterinarian*

KAMUGISHA CHRISTOPHER, *Head of marketing team*

MUSIIME ANABEL, *Head of operations*

NUWAGABA ALBERT, *Head of research*

ABSTRACT Most farmers in Sub-Saharan Africa experience outbreaks of animal viral diseases. The prevalence of outbreaks and the subsequent losses generally reflect the difficulty of detecting the virus.

To increase the contribution of livestock production to national economies—as exports, as imports into manufacturing industries, and as a component of household consumption—animal contagious diseases must be controlled. There is also a need for farmers to derive higher income from livestock in subsistence-oriented economies. To improve detection of foot and mouth disease, we are developing an inexpensive diagnostic device that uses low-power sensors to monitor and communicate results in real time. With this device, there is no cow-flow restriction.

FreshSource: Connecting Farmers to Businesses and Providing Last-Mile Solutions

TEAM FRESHSOURCE

FARAH EMARA, *London School of Economics graduate, 2017*

OMAR EMARA, *University of Bath graduate, 2018*

ABSTRACT Agriculture accounts for nearly 15 percent of the the Arab Republic of Egypt's gross domestic product, 28 percent of all jobs, and more than 15 percent of exports (USAID 2019). Despite its significance, the Egyptian agricultural economy is extremely inefficient. Food loss has reached an all-time high, with more than 30 percent of food produced lost, mostly because of improper handling and storage techniques. The market is plagued with numerous middlemen, who extend the value chain and exploit small farmers.

FreshSource, a mobile e-vendor of agricultural goods, connects farms to businesses and provides last-mile solutions. Farmers who use our services have seen a 25 percent increase in their income, businesses have saved 20 percent, and food loss has been substantially reduced.

The World Bank awarded FreshSource a Digital Agriculture Challenge award. The FreshSource model is critical in creating a zero-hunger world and reaching Sustainable Development Goal (SDG) 2 (ending hunger) and SDG 12 (ensuring sustainable consumption and production patterns).

REFERENCE

USAID (United States Agency for International Development). 2019. "Egypt: Agriculture and Food Security," USAID website, June 14. https://www.usaid.gov/egypt/agriculture-and-food-security.

Golden Banana Syrup: Using Overripe Bananas to Enhance the Production of Glucose Syrup

TEAM GOLDEN BANANA SYRUP

ASHIFA CAHYANI TRISNAPUTRI, *Department of Agronomy, Hasanuddin University, Indonesia*

NANI RAHAYU USMAN, *Department of Food Science and Technology, Hasanuddin University*

MUHAMMAD AL MUSTAWA, *Department of Chemistry, Hasanuddin University*

ABSTRACT Millions of edible bananas are thrown away every day just because they have minor bruises or black marks on their skin after becoming overripe. The emissions from bananas and other landfill waste are 24 times more potent than CO_2 and release methane gas, which is bad for the environment. Using this raw material would eliminate waste, save money, and reduce emissions.

Golden Banana Syrup is a glucose syrup made from overripe bananas. It will be produced using an enzymatic reaction and purification process. Golden Banana Syrup contains 38.27 percent glucose, 1.25 percent protein, 0.1 percent fat, and 151.43 kilocalories. Those results meet the minimum standard for glucose (30 percent), based on reference SNI 01-2978-1992. Using overripe bananas will greatly improve glucose syrup production and help reduce banana waste.

Smart Waste Container: The Automatic Container for Waste Treatment and Sorting

TEAM GOOD WASTE FOR ENVIRONMENTAL SOLUTIONS

ABED ALMAJEED ABU KHALAF, *Founder/CTO*

ABDALLAH SMAIK, *Cofounder/CEO*

MAHMOUD AL-QANNAS, *Electronics officer*

MOHAMMAD SULAIMAN MUSTAFA, *Mechanical designer*

FAHED BASYOUNI, *Marketing officer*

ATIEH FARAJ, *Production officer*

ABSTRACT Like the rest of the world, Jordan suffers from the problem of solid waste and its nondeterioration and spread in the seas and oceans. With the country's high rate of population growth and increasing industrialization, the amount of solid waste has increased, which has put an extra burden on waste management infrastructure. This increase in solid waste leads to unhealthy dumps, which hurt public health and the environment and create socioeconomic problems.

The main problem with recycling is people's lack of awareness, which leads to unsorted waste. Lack of awareness increases the cost of waste sorting, especially for plastic waste. The costs of traditional sorting and recycling are much higher than the cost of producing raw materials.

The Good Waste for Environmental Solutions (GWES) company has innovated a solution to this problem. We have created a smart container that automatically sorts any kind of waste that is thrown into it. The container uses multiple technologies to identify the type of waste and sort it automatically. This innovation includes a catalytic system that rewards users with electronic points that can be exchanged for cash by scanning a QR code using a phone application. In addition, the container will have LCD screens on its sides that can be marketed to businesses as advertising interfaces.

Hilico: An Innovative Portable Rain-Harvesting Device to Provide Slum Dwellers and Disaster Victims with an Efficient, Low-Cost Solution for Clean Water

TEAM HILICO

EYAL YASSKY, *Cofounder and CEO*

MOSHE BELILTY, *Cofounder, mechanical engineer, Afeka College of Engineering, Israel*

ABSTRACT Around the world, 2.1 billion people lack access to clean, safe water. Contaminated water can transmit diseases, such as diarrhea, cholera, dysentery, typhoid, and polio. Contaminated drinking water is estimated to cause 502,000 diarrheal deaths each year. Inequalities exist between and within countries and between the richest and the poorest people within countries. The poor spend up to 50 percent of their income on water (usually of lesser or similar quality)—and they pay much more for it than people who are connected to water infrastructure pay for their water.

The problem is particularly severe in slums, which lack even the surface water sources that are sometimes available in rural areas. Increasing the use of unconventional water sources is vital to escalating progress toward achieving Sustainable Development Goal 6. A key method of achieving this goal is by rain harvesting, a practice that dates back to the emergence of the human race.

For years, our team has been volunteering as disaster-relief mission leaders, looking for ways to use rainwater. Even though about 90 percent of disasters are water related, rainwater is often overlooked as a solution, because almost no efficient harvesting solutions are available in the field. Considering these factors as well as the fact that most of the developing countries affected by severe shortages of clean water also receive tremendous amounts of precipitation, we designed the world's first portable rain-harvesting device. Our lightweight innovation is affordable and efficient for use in slums. The system folds into a small backpack and requires no preexisting infrastructure. It is designed to sustainably provide clean drinking water to off-grid communities and disaster-relief areas worldwide. For a family in the slums of Mumbai, one system can provide most of the water used for cooking and drinking during the entire rainy season.

Iradaa: An Online Platform to Train and Employ People with Disabilities

TEAM IRADAA

AHMED RYAD, *Cofounder/CEO; faculty of mass communication, Cairo University*

MUSTAFA AMIN, *Coordinator/operations associate, media researcher*

SHADY ANWAR, *Technical manager*

NANCY SAAD, *Administrative affairs*

EMAN MAHMOUD, *Commissioner; faculty of mass communication, Cairo University*

MAHMOUD AHMED MOHAMED, *Client services*

ABSTRACT About 15 million people in the Arab Republic of Egypt have disabilities. Most of them are unemployed. Many of these people have skills, and many companies are ready to employ people with disabilities, but companies do not succeed in reaching people with the appropriate competencies. Some civil society organizations provide training, but people with disabilities often do not hear about those opportunities.

Iradaa, an interactive digital online platform, brings together employment agencies, people with disabilities, and training institutions. It is the first platform of its kind in Egypt and the Arab world to bring together the requirements of companies, the potential of people with disabilities, and the available training opportunities. It is designed to be managed by people with disabilities, who know their needs and how they can best be met.

The platform considers accessibility, which facilitates navigation for people with different disabilities. Its service delivery channels include an online website, an application for smart phones, and a hotline.

E-Vigilante: A Low-Cost Self-Regulatory Mechanism for Effluent Monitoring

TEAM JHOR

MOHSHI MASNAD, *Lecturer, Department of Computer Science and Engineering, BRAC University, Bangladesh*

MD. NAFIZ HASAN KHAN, *Graduate student, School of Interactive Arts, Simon Fraser University, Canada*

A.M. ESFAR-E-ALAM, *Lecturer, Department of Computer Science and Engineering, BRAC University, Bangladesh*

DEWAN ZIAUL KARIM, *Lecturer, Department of Computer Science and Engineering, BRAC University, Bangladesh*

ABSTRACT The ready-made garments (RMG) sector is the backbone of Bangladesh's economy. The effluent (wastewater) produced by RMG is directly discharged to surface water, harming the environment and human health. Although Bangladesh's government has imposed stringent rules to control the discharge of effluent directly to surface water, the environment remains vulnerable to pollution because of the lack of a proper and real-time monitoring mechanism from RMG factories and the unwillingness of factory owners to make needed changes. Some real-time remote monitoring systems are available on the market, but most of them are unaffordable.

E-Vigilante is a low-cost, self-regulating mechanism for an online effluent monitoring system. The service targets developing countries such as Bangladesh, where cost is a vital issue. Our proposal provides a detailed analysis of the efficacy of the E-Vigilante system, which monitors various parameters of the effluent directly discharged into surface water. We have incorporated a microcontroller called Arduino and other sensors to develop this open-source water-quality testing system. By engaging current research in open-source water quality systems and embedded systems and conducting a thorough analysis of the current situation in Bangladesh, this proposal develops a strong argument for the strength of E-Vigilante as a practical solution because of its low cost and high efficiency.

LivingWaters: A Portable Three-Step Filtration Process for Rainwater Harvesting

TEAM LIVINGWATERS

JOSHUA KAO, *Founder, inventor, and CEO; structural engineer; marketer; entrepreneur; senior at Rutgers Business School, New Jersey*

JOSEPH BAJOR, *Chief engineer, mechanical engineer, and marketer; senior studying public health at Rutgers University, New Jersey*

ABSTRACT Water is a scarce resource in the region of Rajasthan, India that we surveyed. Existing sources of water are either unable to meet the needs of the people or too contaminated to safely use. As a result, there is a clear demand for an alternative that would cut down the time, effort, and health risks associated with accessing water.

Our solution is a collapsible, portable rainwater harvesting system. Rainwater is the cleanest source of naturally occurring water. By allowing households to collect it from their own roofs, we enable them to maintain a clean source of water right at their doorstep. The unit consists of two tarp gutters that run along the edges of a building, supported by an adjustable drawcord system that allows the unit to support its own weight without being physically attached to the building. It can be set up on any structure with a slanted roof, including less stable temporary structures and tents.

The Living Waters system yields multiple benefits. It requires no special knowledge to set up and maintain. The entire unit can be set up in less than 20 minutes by tossing one side over the roof and adjusting the support ropes to fit. Maintenance is also simple—just remove leaves and twigs from the mesh cover and rinse off the sediment filter occasionally. The device is also portable, which makes it perfect for communities prone to displacement.

Vinsighte: Using Technology to Help Visually Impaired People Achieve Their Full Potential and Live More Comfortable Lives

TEAM VINSIGHTE

KOLAWOLE OLUWATOMISIN, *CEO, University of Ibadan*

MORENIKEJI ERI, *Chief technology officer, University of Ibadan*

OYOLOLA CALEB, *Chief operating officer, University of Ibadan*

DAIRO TOSIN, *Chief information officer, University of Liverpool*

AYANLEYE TOYIN, *Vice president of engineering, University of Ibadan*

ABSTRACT According to the World Health Organization's 2010 global data report, 26.3 million people in Africa are visually impaired; 15 percent of the world's visually impaired population resides in Africa and 32,700 of every 1 million people in the region have visual impairments. Nigeria is estimated to have about 6.5 million visually impaired residents.

People with visual impairments in Africa are neglected and stigmatized; as a result, they struggle to live comfortable lives. Young people are often unable to go to school, and those who try doing so struggle because of their difficulties with reading and navigating the environment independently.

The goal of Vinsighte is to ensure that the visually impaired people in our community live comfortable lives and achieve their full potential. To accomplish this goal, we developed assistive devices that help them read and navigate their environment independently. Our products are Viri and Visis. Viri, a portable handheld walking aid, works by sensing obstacles and obstructions ahead of a visually impaired user and giving feedback via a mild vibration. Visis is a pair of glasses with a camera that uses artificial intelligence to help the wearer read by converting the texts of books to audio.

With our technology, stigmatization of visually impaired people would be reduced, young visually impaired individuals would have access to education, and the quality of life and well-being of the visually impaired community would greatly improve.

WASE: Circular Wastewater and Fecal Sludge Management for Decentralized Treatment

TEAM WASE

THOMAS FUDGE, *CEO, PhD researcher, Brunel University, London*

LLŶR WILLIAMS, *Chief operating officer, 2018 graduate, Brunel University, London*

WILLIAM GAMBIER, *Chief technology officer, 2018 graduate, Brunel University, London*

ABSTRACT About 2.3 billion people lack suitable sanitation, and 80 percent of wastewater worldwide is dumped into the environment untreated. Obstacles to waste treatment often relate to the high capital costs necessary for centralized sewerage systems, which also have high operational costs and energy demands.

WASE is developing a revolutionary electro-methanogenic reactor (EMR) technology so that we can offer decentralized wastewater treatment. We provide a circular approach, using wastewater to generate biogas, produce fertilizers, and recover water for reuse. Our technology integrates into urban communities as well as industrial applications, creating opportunities for onsite waste management and energy generation. Our modular EMR system creates a Lego brick approach to wastewater management. Our innovation allows customization, enabling users to treat toilet waste directly. It can be scaled up for community decentralized wastewater treatment plants or treatment of industrial wastewater from agriculture or food and drink manufacturers.

The system provides significant benefits over existing solutions. It treats waste 10 times faster than anaerobic digestion (AD), with higher chemical oxygen demand (COD) removal rates (<125mg/L COD) and biogas methane concentrations up to 80 percent (20 percent higher than AD). With a return on investment of three to five years, the system generates savings for users while providing secure and affordable sustainable energy and wastewater management solutions.